Fund
Libra

Fundamentals of Library Supervision

Fundamentals of Library Supervision

SECOND EDITION

Joan Giesecke and Beth McNeil

AMERICAN LIBRARY ASSOCIATION
CHICAGO 2010

Joan Giesecke is professor and dean of libraries at the University of Nebraska–Lincoln. She joined the university in 1987 and became dean in 1996. She has held positions at George Mason University, Prince George's County Memorial Library System, and the American Health Care Association. She received a doctorate in public administration from George Mason University, an M.L.S. degree from the University of Maryland, and a master's degree in management from Central Michigan University. Giesecke is a former editor of *Library Administration and Management Journal* and has published numerous articles on management issues. Her books include *Practical Help for New Supervisors* (1997), *Scenario Planning for Libraries* (1998), *Practical Strategies for Library Managers* (2001), and *Academic Librarians as Emotionally Intelligent Leaders* (2008).

Beth McNeil is professor and associate dean for academic affairs at Purdue University Libraries, where she is responsible for public services, collections, and scholarly communication. Prior to joining Purdue in 2007, McNeil was associate dean of libraries at the University of Nebraska–Lincoln, where she led technical services operations, coordinated the staff development program, and coordinated library-wide statistics efforts. She received an M.S. degree in library and information science from the University of Illinois at Urbana-Champaign. Her books include *Patron Behavior in Libraries* (1996) and *Human Resource Management in Today's Academic Library* (2004).

The paper used in this publication meets the minimum requirements of American National Standard for Information Sciences—Permanence of Paper for Printed Library Materials, ANSI Z39.48-1992. ⊗

Library of Congress Cataloging-in-Publication Data
    Giesecke, Joan.
        Fundamentals of library supervision / Joan Giesecke and Beth McNeil. — 2nd ed.
            p.   cm. — (ALA fundamentals series)
        Includes bibliographical references and index.
        ISBN 978-0-8389-1016-0 (alk. paper)
        1. Library personnel management—United States. 2. Supervision of employees.
    I. McNeil, Beth. II. Title.
        Z682.2.U5G54 2010
        023'.9—dc22   2009028890

ISBN-13: 978-0-8389-1016-0

Printed in the United States of America

14   13   12   11   10   5   4   3   2   1

Contents

Additional material can be found on the book's website,
at www.ala.org/editions/extras/giesecke10160.
Look for website material wherever you see this symbol:

Figures

Several of the figures can be downloaded from the book's website, at www.ala.org/editions/extras/giesecke10160.

Preface

MANAGEMENT USED TO be simple. The manager or supervisor told employees what to do and employees did what they were told. That world does not exist today. Today's managers, supervisors, team leaders, project managers, and unit heads face a more complex environment. Managers need to balance production goals with concern for people issues in a continually changing setting. The workplace and the workforce are different. Managers may now find themselves overseeing four generations of staff, each with its own characteristics and needs. Each group responds best to a different management style. Additionally, more women are in management roles, bringing a different perspective to the administration of organizations.

The legal environment is also more complex, with laws addressing discrimination, sexual harassment, health issues, and other personnel issues. Today's supervisor needs to keep up with legal changes if he or she is to avoid legal challenges.

As this book goes to press, the bleak economic climate dominates the news. Supervisors may be facing reductions in forces, layoffs, furloughs, or pay cuts. At the same time, use of library services may be increasing as the public turns to libraries for Internet access and job-hunting services, as well as recreational reading, media, and computer games. In these difficult times, good supervisory skills are essential. Supervisors must take a leadership role in providing support for their staff and ensuring the library can meet its goals and objectives. Poor supervisory skills will only compound the morale problems that arise during difficult times. Excellent supervisory skills can lead to departments and units that not only cope with the challenges they face, but are able to move forward and become excellent organizations.

While our world is more complicated, it is also more exciting. Managers have more flexibility in how they structure their units or organizations. They have more options for delegating tasks, establishing goals, and encouraging staff development. They can build high-powered teams that surpass traditionally structured units.

How can supervisors and managers create an exciting environment? Many of the fundamentals of management that lead to a productive workplace are basic common sense. Others require taking a new view of management and letting go of the idea of central control.[1] In this book, we cover the fundamentals of good management and bring together practical advice from experts with basic commonsense approaches to solving today's management challenges. Whether you are a new supervisor just getting started or an experienced manager, you will find that the topics covered here provide you with an overview and foundation for the tasks and responsibilities of being a manager.

This book explains getting started as a supervisor or manager, creating a positive working environment, managing teams, working with a diverse workforce, and recognizing fundamental legal issues that arise in today's workplace. Practical skills that are covered include hiring, interviewing, orienting, and appraising employees; managing rewards; and planning and organizing work. Project management, meetings management, and communication skills are also discussed.

Throughout the book, examples of supervisory challenges will be exemplified through the experience of two new supervisors. Gina is the head of a reference unit who was hired from outside the organization. Tony is the head of a cataloging unit and was promoted from within the organization. Their different perspectives will help illustrate ways that supervisors can address the various tasks and challenges their jobs entail. The examples and stories in this book are composites created from a variety of experiences and organizations. All names, circumstances, and details have been altered. Any resemblance to real people is coincidental.

If you enjoy bringing people together and helping them do their best, you are ready to be a manager. Enjoy the complexities and challenges that make up this very exciting world.

NOTE

1. Camila Alire, "Two Intriguing Practices to Library Management Theory," *Library Administration and Management* 18, no. 1 (Winter 2004): 39–41.

1

Today's Workplace

Trends

Changing Roles of Managers and Supervisors

Changing Competencies

Leadership Skills

Summary

TODAY'S MANAGERS FACE a workplace that is significantly different from the one that existed even a few years ago. Today's world is more fast-paced, and change is a way of life. The global economic recession of 2008 and 2009 has shown how vulnerable all organizations are to the impact of economic instability. Increasing unemployment, decreasing state and local revenues, and increasing uncertainty about the future are compli-cating the planning process for any organization. Organizations face new competition, changing technology, mergers and acquisitions, bankrupt-cies, changing consumer expectations, and economic instability in the normal course of events. They work in a global environment, with poten-tial suppliers and customers located anywhere. Jobs are being outsourced to offshore companies and third world nations. Multinational companies are learning how to blend cultures and develop management structures that can be successful in multiple environments. Technological changes impact all aspects of business, from financial systems to human resources and knowledge-base systems. Trying to keep up with the many changes in how technology can be used is a full-time job. Furthermore, managers are faced with the instability that can result from mergers and acquisitions, as well as from the blending of different types of organizations within the same industry. Managing becomes more challenging when you are not sure if the top management of the company is arranging a restructuring or planning to sell the company to another owner. Long-range plans quickly become short-range strategies for survival if you don't think you have a long time frame to protect your own career. To compound this uncertainty, today's managers also face an uncertain economic environment, with budget reductions, downsizing, and restructuring of financial plans having become facts of life. Externally, organizations face the challenge of new expectations from customers who want to customize anything they can, including restaurant meals, and want everything quickly. Satisfying customer demands when those demands are always changing compounds the challenges of planning and organizing work for effectiveness and efficiency. The changing political landscape is also making planning for librarians more challenging. The election of the first African American president, Barack Obama, in November 2008 signaled a potential change in how the federal government approaches regulations, economic recovery, and military activities. Librarians will need to carefully assess how federal regulations on information infrastructure change, if at all, and how these changes impact what libraries can and cannot do to protect the privacy of their patrons and support core library values.

Trends

Libraries are not immune to these different forces, and library managers need to understand how these forces and other trends impact their organizations.[1]

Competition. Libraries face competition from a variety of sources, including the most obvious source, Google. Today's students, citizens, or company employees are more likely to try Google first for information than they are to check with a librarian. Library patrons can also be found studying in bookstores with cafés and comfortable seating rather than in public, school, or academic libraries. Libraries are trying to look more like bookstores and cafés even while people abandon bookstores for libraries as the economy worsens. Library managers need to understand this world of competition if they are to position their libraries to remain a vital part of their communities or organizations.

Competition has forced librarians into becoming marketing managers, learning how to advertise and market their services. No longer can libraries afford to sit back and assume that everyone knows what libraries can contribute to the community. Instead, librarians must develop plans to explain why libraries are still needed and why they play a vital role in the information-rich world we live in. The American Library Association's @ your library campaign is one of many ways libraries can market their services and advertise their worth. As libraries face budget reductions, librarians need to actively solicit community support and demonstrate how they can contribute to the economic and social well-being of their community or campus, if they are to avoid becoming irrelevant.

Technology. Changing technology is a way of life in today's libraries. The library manager who waits to find the perfect system before implementing new technologies will not be successful. Librarians have to become risk takers, trying new technologies even though the results are not guaranteed. Moreover, managers must let go of the idea that once a decision on technology has been made and hardware and software have been purchased, they can keep that technology for a long time. Hardware and software change regularly, and libraries must find ways to remain current if the library is to remain vital to its patrons. Finding funds to upgrade workstations on a three-year cycle, for example, will change how budgets are structured and how priorities are set.

Mobile technology is changing how patrons communicate. Information is available anytime, anywhere, on one's BlackBerry, iPhone, or other mobile device. Libraries appear as physical spaces, websites, RSS feeds, blogs, Facebook pages, or as a part of the search toolbar. Patrons in the library may instant message (IM) a reference desk that is located just a few feet from where they are sitting rather than get up to ask a question. All of these changes alter how librarians think about services and service delivery.

Technology changes also impact internal organizational structures. With networked resources and online systems available in many libraries, managers may find that their staff include employees who want to telecommute rather than work on-site. Supervising these employees takes careful planning and creativity to ensure that productivity measures are met and that these staff feel a part of the overall unit or department. The use of technology also brings ergonomic concerns to the workplace, with supervisors now needing to address issues of safe workplaces and workstation arrangements that will decrease the chances of staff developing health problems such as carpal tunnel syndrome. While previously any table or chair might do, today's workers who spend all day working at computers need a work space that can be adjusted to meet their individual needs. Furthermore, ubiquitous network options and handheld devices mean that employees can be connected to their workplace and their e-mail no matter where they may be located physically. Work time can expand to include any time of the day or night. Supervisors and managers now need to address the issue of staff who may work too many off-hours, complicating the discussion of what constitutes work and work-related activities.

Technology also impacts how decisions can be made. Supervisors may now have access to a variety of data on workload, productivity, and customer satisfaction that they might not have had twenty years ago. They can use computer systems to monitor productivity measures such as how long staff take to catalog or process items, as well as how long someone takes to answer a question on a chat reference service. Data can make decision making more transparent, or it can be used by some to obscure how decisions are actually made.

Mergers and acquisitions. While most libraries do not think about mergers as a major force in the field, changes in organizational structures are occurring. Public and school libraries are being blended in the same space. Corporations are centralizing information services, eliminating smaller local collections and services. Academic libraries are closing branches and building virtual libraries instead of physical collections in order to serve dispersed populations. Granted, these types of changes have occurred at various times in the history of libraries. But today, with economic uncertainties and the changing information world, managers may face situations that they never thought would impact their institutions.

Customer expectations. Libraries know that customer expectations have changed. Customers want access to a wide variety of information resources and services at times that are convenient for them. Libraries that are not customer-focused will not be supported and will find that their funding suffers.

Economic uncertainty. Libraries are all too familiar with the problems of budget and staffing reductions. In tough economic times, libraries may be seen as less central to the core mission of an organization, less central to the core activities of a school, and less important to a state, county, or city that has to pay for mandated initiatives and social programs. For example, in a recent survey of citizens in Lincoln, Nebraska, on their perceptions of city services, citizens rated libraries as essential services. Nonetheless, when asked to prioritize the funding of city services, citizens rated fire and police as essential and libraries as nice but not crucial for the city.[2]

Changing workforce. Perhaps the most noticeable trend is the changing demographics in the United States. The population is becoming more diverse. Libraries need to learn to recruit and retain staff from a variety of ethnic and racial backgrounds. Another change in demographics is the changing generations in the workplace, with four generations of workers now a part of many of our institutions. Supervisors can no longer assume that all employees will behave and react to the environment in the same way. Many of today's newer employees are interested first in what they can get out of a job rather than being focused on how they can contribute to the organization. Supervisors need to think about how to build partnerships with staff to get the work done rather than thinking they can simply give orders and have staff carry out those orders.

Global economy. While many libraries may think of themselves as local institutions, libraries are still connected to and influenced by the global economy. With the many mergers in the publishing field, libraries are buying many of their reference and scholarly resources from companies headquartered in Europe and other countries. Acquisition budget planning has to include the impact of exchange rates as well as the impact of inflation.

Libraries and publishers are also taking advantage of the global economy by outsourcing digitization work to countries such as China and India, where labor costs are less than in the United States. Partnerships are being created, too, as libraries join with libraries in other countries to provide online real-time reference assistance on a twenty-four-hour basis. These partnerships are helping libraries expand services to meet the demand for service in a 24/7 world.

Today's library managers and supervisors need to be aware of these trends and how they will impact their own institutions and organizations. Every manager has to understand the big picture of the information field if she is to be successful in an environment of change.

Changing Roles of Managers and Supervisors

Not only are the organizations we work in changing, but the role of the supervisor is also changing. In the mid-twentieth century, the manager's role could be described by the acronym POSDCoRB, which stands for

Planning. Managers were responsible for determining organization goals and deciding how the organization should meet those goals.

Organizing. Managers determined how the work would be divided among organizational units and decided what procedures would be used to accomplish those tasks.

Staffing. Managers were responsible for the personnel decisions in their units, including hiring and evaluating staff.

Directing. Managers directed the work of others, deciding who would complete which tasks.

Coordinating. Managers coordinated activities between units. Staff were responsible only for work within their own units.

Reporting. Managers were responsible for reporting on unit accomplishments and keeping upper management informed about unit progress.

Budgeting. Managers were responsible for the unit's budget, determining how resources would be divided and monitoring to make sure that budgets were met.

While these roles still exist in our organizations, it is more likely that in today's environment these activities are shared between the supervisors and the staff. A supervisor is more coach than director and more facilitator than commander. New roles for supervisors include recognizing and recruiting talent, teaching staff new skills and promoting learning, understanding the organization's culture, and understanding organizational power.

Talent. Successful supervisors are learning new ways to recruit. They are learning that they need to recruit talent and ability rather than looking only at skills. Supervisors know they can teach skills to talented employees easier than they can teach talent to someone. Without the key talents and abilities needed to do a job, a staff member is unlikely to excel. In today's market, where recruiting is very competitive, it is important to recruit the best staff possible so the unit can succeed and grow.

Promoting learning. Most staff today want a job that provides personal satisfaction, where they can control their own destinies, and where they have a voice in what happens.[3] In organizations that promote learning and encourage staff development, staff are more likely to find the satisfaction they seek. Supervisors who promote a partnership approach to the management of the unit are more likely to create an environment where staff have input in the unit and feel appreciated for their efforts.

Organizational culture. Successful supervisors understand the organizational culture in which they operate. Supervisors need to know how the organization measures success, how rewards are determined, how mistakes are handled, how decisions are made, and how risk is tolerated. They also understand the time frame in which the organization operates. Some libraries, for example, work on a semester system, some on the school year, and some on the fiscal year. These time frames impact how objectives are measured and how the pace of the work is likely to be set.

Supervisors can learn their organization's culture by carefully listening to others, observing how things are done, keeping an open mind about workflow and processes, observing who succeeds and why, and remembering to look at the big picture beyond their own units. Setting aside time to reflect on organizational activities and keeping notes on what works and what does not work will help identify the key elements in the culture.

Power. Power is a natural part of an organization. Supervisors should review the organizational chart to see how their units fit into the overall structure and fit with each other. It also helps to identify what activities are not reflected on the organizational chart and then learn how these functions are dispersed in the organization. Understanding relationships will also help in identifying organizational politics. It helps, for example, to know if colleagues were sorority sisters or fraternity brothers. Do they belong to the same groups? Do these people form an alliance in the organization? How does the distribution of power in the organization relate to the political relationships? Thinking explicitly about the organization and reflecting upon what goes on will give supervisors a better chance of developing ways to work that are successful and are rewarded.

Changing Competencies

Managers and supervisors need to develop a variety of competencies beyond technical expertise to succeed in their jobs with these new roles and responsibilities. The soft skills of human resources management, team building, and leadership are the foundation of successful management at all levels of the organization. Plan on putting the following competencies to work daily as you develop your skills as a manager.[4]

Interpersonal skills. Supervision is about creating relationships. Good people skills are a must.

Communication skills. Written, verbal, and active listening communication skills are crucial.

Problem solving and decision making. Learning to analyze data and using that data to resolve problems will help you work effectively. Using good judgment is also a key success factor.

Initiative. Taking the initiative, anticipating needs, and taking action are the signs of a good supervisor.

Delegation. Learning to appropriately delegate the right tasks to the right people is a skill that is often overlooked. Take time to learn how to delegate effectively.

Time management. Managing your own time as well as the time of your staff will make your unit more successful and able to complete assigned projects and tasks.

Meetings management. Much of the work in today's organizations is done through groups and teams. Knowing how to run an efficient and effective meeting will make your groups more successful. Ensuring that meetings are not seen as an alternative to work and as a waste of time and effort is an important skill.

Customer service. Know the needs of your patrons, your internal customers, and your external constituencies and be sure everyone in your unit is focused on how they can meet those needs. Service is everyone's business.

Leadership Skills

Leadership skills are no longer solely the purview of upper management. Today, all supervisors and managers need to understand and demonstrate good leadership skills. These skills or strategies help managers keep up with change as they prepare their employees for new roles and new challenges. In the book *Creating Magic: 10 Common Sense Leadership Strategies from a Life at Disney,* Lee Cockerell describes the ten leadership strategies that the Disney corporation found to be most effective. These strategies are particularly applicable to service industries such as libraries where customer or patron satisfaction is a key success factor.[5]

Strategy one: value your employees. As a supervisor, you want to develop an inclusive style that values every employee in your unit and in your organization. Cockerell uses the acronym RAVE to describe this strategy: respect, appreciate, and value everyone.[6] In *The One Minute Manager,* Ken Blanchard and Spenser Johnson refer to this as "catch them doing something right."[7] Be sure you sincerely thank staff for a job well done. Staff will know if you are only going through the motions of being sincere and will resent your efforts.

Strategy two: look for creative change strategies. As a supervisor, you want to keep asking how you can improve on processes and structure. How can you make the unit a better, more effective one? What types of creative changes will bring the best results? By being open to new ideas you will be more likely to see possible changes that will bring positive results.

Strategy three: hire the best. Perhaps the most important decisions you make as a manager or a supervisor are hiring decisions, because your staff become the embodiment of your brand. That is, customers will judge your area by the response they get from your staff. You want to hire the best talent you can. As noted in *First, Break All the Rules,* hire talent and train for skills.[8] You can teach someone new skills, but you cannot teach them to be talented. When you have good people working for you, your unit will be successful. If you have to spend most of your time correcting hiring errors, your unit will not be able to excel.

Strategy four: training is key. Providing training for your unit is essential. If your institution has a staff development program, be sure your staff are taking advantage of training opportunities. If your organization does not provide this type of support, look for training opportunities you can bring to your unit. Is there a webinar available on a particular process or challenge your unit is facing? Is there someone in your community who can help with skill building? Be creative as you look for opportunities to coach your staff to excel.

Strategy five: eliminate hassles. Look for ways that you can make processes and procedures more streamlined and effective for your patrons and your staff. Try being a customer in your own library. Can you easily fill out an online form for a service? Can you find the information you need to answer a reference question? You may also want to borrow ideas from other service organizations. Have you experienced great service? What made the experience so successful? Are there elements of the service that you can bring to your unit?

Strategy six: learn the truth, then act. In the 1970s, management literature referred to management by walking around. Get out of your office and out from behind your desk and find out what is going on in your unit. When someone brings you a problem, listen carefully and get the whole story. Verify facts before you act so that you are sure you are working with the best information possible before you determine how to resolve an issue. You will be in a better position to assess information that staff bring to you when you have a thorough and current understanding of the activities in your unit.

Strategy seven: reward the behaviors you want to see. Reward the behaviors you want and do not encourage the behaviors that should be eliminated. Too often supervisors either ignore poor performance or spend so much time trying to correct a problem that they forget to reward and encourage those who are performing well. Do not take your best employees for granted. Instead, recognize and encourage excellence. You will find that you get the behaviors you reward.

Strategy eight: keep learning. In a world of change, supervisors and managers need to keep an open mind and seek new ideas and innovations if they are to be successful. You need to stay current on trends, learn what others in the field are doing to meet the challenges of the day, and seek to implement best practices. As Cockerell notes, "it is the learners who inherit the future. The learned . . . live in a world that no longer exists."[9] To avoid trying to manage the past, become an active learner.

Strategy nine: always be professional. In this day and age, that one picture of you with a lamp shade on your head is likely to appear on the Internet. The sarcastic remark on your Facebook page will be shared with all your colleagues. As a professional you will want to be sure you project an appropriate image. That image does not include arrogance. Remember that humility is a key ingredient in professionalism.[10] When you treat your staff with respect and value their expertise, you will have a strong, well-functioning unit that will excel.

Strategy ten: be an ethical manager. Leading with integrity is important if you want your staff to commit to the unit and to support you. You are also responsible for teaching positive values to your unit and creating a culture of inclusiveness.

Summary

Change is simply a way of life for the library and information field. While the core functions of libraries—providing an organized collection of materials and providing assistance in using those materials—remain the same, how libraries fulfill those functions is being transformed. Technological advances make it possible for libraries to provide access to a wide range of materials that no single library owns. Libraries can serve customers from around the world as easily as they serve the patrons who enter their buildings.

In such a world, managers in today's libraries must embrace change. The management strategies that worked many years ago are not successful in today's volatile environment. Managers and supervisors need to stay aware of the many trends that impact the library field and learn how to bring the best of these changes into their units and organizations. Successful managers will be those who have learned to navigate in the white water of the library and information field while supervising employees who make herding cats look easy.

NOTES

1. For an overview of current trends and their impact on the library field, see *2003 OCLC Environmental Scan: Pattern Recognition* (Dublin, OH: OCLC, 2004).
2. University of Nebraska Public Policy Center, "Priority Lincoln: Budgeting for Outcomes" (May 29, 2008), p. 32; http://ppc.nebraska.edu/project/BudgetngOutcomesandPrioritiesLincoln/reports/PriorityLincolnFinalReport.pdf.
3. Gary McClain and Deborah S. Romaine, *The Everything Managing People Book* (Avon, MA: Adams Media, 2002), 11.
4. William A. Salmon, *The New Supervisor's Survival Manual* (New York: AMACOM, 1999), 5–7.
5. Lee Cockerell, *Creating Magic: 10 Common Sense Leadership Strategies from a Life at Disney* (New York: Doubleday, 2008), 54–55.
6. Ibid.
7. Ken Blanchard and Spenser Johnson, *The One Minute Manager* (New York: Morrow, 1982).
8. Marcus Buckingham and Curt Coffman, *First, Break All the Rules* (New York: Simon and Schuster, 1999), 67.
9. Cockerell, *Creating Magic,* 208.
10. Ibid., 44.

Becoming a Manager

GINA HAS JUST started work as the head of reference at the local university. She was recruited from another state institution and is looking forward to working at the university. Gina has lots of questions about the unit and is just getting started when there is a knock on her door. Phil, an experienced member of the reference department, enters. Gina smiles hello. Phil begins to explain how he should have gotten the job as the senior member of the department. He leaves Gina feeling a bit confused. Other members stop in to introduce themselves and to wish her luck. Looking at the disarray in the office, Gina figures she will need all the luck she can get.

Tony has started work as the head of cataloging the same day Gina joined the reference department. Tony was promoted from within the department. On his first day, staff drop by to congratulate Tony and to voice concerns. Bottlenecks have been occurring between cataloging and acquisitions, and the head of acquisitions wants to know what Tony is going to do to solve this problem. Another colleague drops in to repeat her long-standing concern about having an adjustable chair for her desk. What is Tony going to do about this?

By the end of the day, Gina and Tony both understand just exactly what they have gotten into. Both thought supervisor positions would give them more time to look at policies and help implement a vision for the

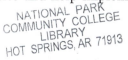

unit. Instead, they each spent the day on minute details that others should have been able to handle. How are they each going to turn around the units to make them functional, productive parts of the operation? Welcome to the world of supervision and management.

If the above day sounds intriguing, you are thinking like a manager. Gina and Tony are quickly discovering that management is not about technical skills. Rather, it is about helping others accomplish their tasks, solving problems, developing staff, and creating a positive working environment. Gina and Tony have their work cut out for them. Each must change his or her own perspective, learn to see the unit differently, and learn how the job has now changed. They could use some training, advice, and help.

Let's explore what it takes to be a supervisor, head, or manager of a unit, department, or organization.

Competencies

What are the core competencies for today's supervisors and managers? What are the skills, knowledge, and personal attributes that contribute to your success as a manager? If you think that the ability to give commands and control your unit will make you successful, you will be disappointed. Today's supervisors must move beyond the command and control mentality to develop skills in coaching, facilitation, and negotiation. You will need to be customer-focused, able to support and implement change in response to the changing information environment, and able to work in or lead teams and groups, while ensuring that your unit is productive and meets organizational goals and objectives.

Supervisory or managerial competencies can be divided into a number of groups.[1] Key skills that are the foundation for any position include technical competence, oral and written communication skills, and time management skills. In addition, supervisors, managers, and other members of the organization should support diversity, demonstrate flexibility, and exhibit self-awareness.

Next, supervisors need to have good problem-solving and decision-making skills and be able to manage conflict and build teams. Supervisors also need to demonstrate personnel management skills, including coaching and developing staff, setting standards and expectations, and conducting performance reviews.

As one advances in management, planning and budgeting skills become more important. Negotiating among units or departments also becomes a part of one's role. Finally, thinking about the organization as a whole and working to develop and achieve organizational goals round out the manager's role.

Supervisors not only need to demonstrate these competencies themselves, but are also responsible for coaching staff to help them develop these important competencies.

Myths versus Reality

Besides building new competencies, supervisors need to let go of a number of myths about management that no longer apply to today's workplace.[2]

Myth: You are in charge of everything. *Reality:* If you think about this statement, you will realize that you cannot be in charge of every detail in your unit. Staff continually make decisions about their tasks, procedures, and work. If they did not make decisions, they would not be doing their jobs. As a manager, you are responsible for seeing that the work is done, and while you want to be sure you pitch in and help when needed, you are not doing your staff any favors if you try to do their work in addition to your own.

Myth: You cannot trust your staff. *Reality:* This myth assumes that staff are not going to do their jobs well and that management must spend time preventing poor performance. This attitude is not helpful in today's workplace, where building motivated teams of staff who take pride in their work is an important part of creating a productive, positive environment. If you do not trust your staff, ask yourself why you hired them and why you are retaining them. Instead of assuming the worst, assume you have talented staff until that is proven false.

Myth: You cannot show emotion as a manager. *Reality:* Although management theorists in the 1970s advised that managers should not show emotion, today's successful manager knows that managing emotions or emotional intelligence is an important part of her responsibilities. Emotional intelligence includes the two core ideas of "the ability to manage one's own emotions and the ability to understand and recognize the emotions of others."[3] By managing one's own emotions, a manager can establish a positive working environment that centers on respect for all. By recognizing the emotions of others, a manager can adjust her style and reactions to limit negativity and promote a constructive response to a given situation.

Myth: You must always defend your staff. *Reality:* Perhaps one of the hardest things to learn as a new manager is that you need to support your staff and still recognize when performance issues have to be addressed. For example, if Gina in the reference unit is told by her boss that patrons are complaining about the poor treatment they receive at the desk, then Gina needs to investigate the complaint and work to improve the service in the department rather than spend time defending her staff to her boss without knowing if the complaints are valid or not.

Myth: You always have to be right. *Reality:* As a manager, you need to learn to admit when you made a mistake and take action to correct the problem. If you assume you must always be right, then you may ignore information that runs counter to your own beliefs. You also need to learn when to compromise and back down from a position that is no longer valid. Learning to see the big picture and recognizing when you can learn from others is an important part of being a manager.

Roles

Letting go of these ideas about management will help you, as a supervisor, be open to taking on new roles and approaches to managing your unit. As a supervisor, you will have a number of new roles.[4] These roles include

mentor to your staff

facilitator for managing conflict

monitor of your unit's performance

coordinator of projects

planner for your unit

creator working productively with your staff

broker and negotiator for your unit

innovator for managing change

Style

To carry out these roles, Gina and Tony will need to develop an appropriate management style. At first, Tony may think that success will come as long as everyone likes him, as they did when he was a colleague. All he needs to do is keep people happy. But if Tony follows this path, he will soon find that happy staff are not necessarily productive staff. Gina may think that the same skills that make a good parent make a good supervisor. But treating her staff as one would treat children also will not be effective. The workplace is populated with adults, and Gina needs to treat her staff as adults.

Management styles can be described in terms of staff concern and task concern.[5] A manager who is concerned with tasks but not concerned with people will be very autocratic. This command and control approach, common in the early twentieth century, was a one-way process where decisions were made by the manager and staff needs were ignored. While minimal work got done, the environment did not foster excellence. Today's staff are more likely to rebel and leave rather than stay in a stifling work environment.

A manager who is concerned about staff but not tasks is out to win a popularity contest. This manager makes decisions to make people happy. Conflicts are smoothed over rather than resolved. While staff may be happy, they are not likely to be challenged to do their best.

A manager who avoids both task and people issues basically abdicates any responsibility for the unit. Here there is little or no communication, conflict is avoided, and only safe decisions are made. The absentee manager leaves the unit to fend for itself.

Finally, the manager who is concerned about people and productivity will seek to create an environment that encourages people to do their best. Communication is two-way, conflicts are resolved, and staff are encouraged to grow and develop. These managers are most likely to create a positive working environment.

To be effective, Gina and Tony need to develop styles that balance concern for tasks with concern for people. If and when they can balance these two elements, they will be more likely to succeed.

As Gina finishes her first day, she may find the list of roles, skills, and abilities overwhelming. How can Gina begin to establish herself as a supervisor even as she works to develop other skills needed to do the job?

The Manager's View

One of the things that Tony has to learn as a supervisor is that his view or perspective on the organization needs to change. He is no longer one of the staff members. He needs to have an understanding of the whole unit and how his unit fits into the organization. He needs to develop relations with other supervisors, with his staff, and with his boss.

Gina and Tony will find that a manager's job is filled with ambiguity. It is an open-ended job that never seems to end. Facing multiple, unrelated problems ranging from the insignificant to the important is part of a typical manager's day. Gina and Tony will find that a manager's job is no longer about being a producer of services. Nor will either of them be an expert for a particular service or task. Rather, they will find that they need to know a little about a lot of tasks. Breadth replaces depth of knowledge. Therefore, Gina and Tony must learn to rely on staff to be the experts. They will need to trust staff to know the intricacies of each task, while they themselves will need to understand how all the tasks fit together. They will come to see that management is a position of interdependence, because managers need to guide their staff to excel even as they depend on them to make the unit a success.[6]

Many new managers may be surprised at how their views must change if they are to be successful. As Gina and Tony are solving problems and handling daily crises or putting out fires, they need to get to know their respective staff from the perspective of a supervisor. Whether you are promoted from within or hired outside the library, as a new supervisor it is important to get to know each staff member as an individual. In the first few weeks on the job, you should set aside time to meet with each staff member in order to listen to his or her concerns. This is not the time for a lecture. Rather, this is a supervisor's best opportunity to establish a new working relationship with each member of the unit. In these conversations, ask open-ended questions about each person's job. This will help encourage staff to share their ideas and concerns. You can find out what people like about their jobs, what things are challenging to them, and what things they might like to see changed. You will want to keep the conversation friendly and work-related. This is not an informal, social conversation. It is an important, work-related conversation that will help you, as a supervisor, begin to understand the intricacies and complexities of the unit. It is also important to ask each person the same question to start the conversation. Sending out two or three questions ahead of the meeting will give staff a chance to think about what they want to say. Using the same questions as a starting point will assure staff that they are all being treated in a similar manner. Even though each conversation will be different, starting out in a similar way will let staff control what other types of information they want to share initially.

Building a Relationship with Your Boss

Gina and Tony also need to have a series of conversations with their respective bosses in order to learn how they fit into the overall organization. As a reference manager, Gina may well be part of an overall public services division. She will want to find out how her unit's work impacts the work of other units in the division. For example, if interlibrary loan is part of the circulation unit, but the reference desk answers questions for interlibrary loan materials, then Gina will want to confirm what the expectations are for her unit regarding interlibrary loan material. Gina and Tony will also want to clarify performance expectations with their bosses. To continue the above example, Gina needs to know how quickly interlibrary loan requests are filled so her unit can give accurate information to patrons about the service. Clarifying expectations in the beginning will help Gina set a positive tone for working with her boss.

In establishing a working relationship with your new boss, think about the kind of employee you want working for you and determine how you can be that same type of employee for your boss. Key characteristics of a productive employer-employee relationship include the following ones.[7]

Supportive. Look for ways to support your boss, your organization, and your organization's policies and procedures. Think about what you can do to ensure that policies are implemented in your unit and that your unit is contributing to organization goals.

Positive. Bring a positive and respectful attitude to work. While your boss is not always right, nor would you want to follow him blindly, you will want to begin with the assumption that the boss knows what he is doing. A positive attitude also includes watching your own moods. Although we are not likely to be cheerful every day, it is important to not pout about every little mishap. An even-tempered approach to the workplace will go a long way to creating a positive, productive environment and a good working relationship with your boss.

Good work habits. You set the tone for your unit. When you arrive on time, do not take excessively long breaks, and keep a neat work area, you send a signal to your boss that you care about your job. You send the same signal to your unit.

Willingness to learn. In today's changing information environment, it is crucial that we are always ready and willing to learn new things. Look for ways to increase knowledge of your job, your unit, and your organization. You can help your unit stay up-to-date in this changing field while showing your boss that you care about improving your unit.

Complete assigned work on time. While you spend a lot of time as a supervisor building relationships and interacting with your staff, it is also important to make sure that assigned tasks are completed. When your boss asks for a report, or paperwork is due, get it done on time.

Work well with others. Your boss will look to you to build good working relationships with other supervisors in the department and in the organization. Look for ways to build networks and avoid the "us vs. them" syndrome.

Building a Working Relationship with Your Peers

Gina and Tony also need to begin building working relationships with their peers. Their peers are other supervisors in their units and in the organization. This is their new group of colleagues. If they see their peers as competitors, they will find it difficult to build supportive relationships. They may see the actions of other units as threats to their own groups. They may become defensive around other managers. Such an approach will likely lead to conflict and failure.

As a supervisor new to the library, Gina will soon learn that her peers are her main support group. Other supervisors can provide advice on how to handle problems, how the organization functions, and how to succeed in the organization. They can help Gina see things from a different perspective and help her formulate plans.

Gina and Tony may also find it useful to get to know each other as new supervisors and to compare experiences. When you are new to any organization, it can be very helpful to talk to other new people to learn about their efforts within the institution or organization. New supervisors may be more willing to talk more openly among themselves in a group that will not be evaluating their work as closely as a boss or members of their department. Working together, new supervisors can also divide the time it takes to get answers to common questions and to share these answers with the group. By dividing up orientation tasks among themselves, supervisors can benefit from each other's expertise as they learn about the organization.

Unfortunately, some colleagues will not be interested in creating a positive working environment. They may be disillusioned, long-term employees who resist change. Gina will need to recognize this negative behavior and avoid letting someone else's negative view of the organization influence her attitude. Gina cannot change these people, but she can take steps to prevent them from spreading their negative view to her unit.

As a supervisor promoted from within, Tony will need to develop a new relationship with other supervisors. He may have to remind some people that he is a supervisor. He can also benefit from having face-to-face meetings with his new peers to find out how their units work and how they can develop new partnerships.

As Gina and Tony develop good working relationships with their peers and build a lateral team in the organization, they will be better able to expand their views of the organization and to work to integrate their unit into the department or institution.

Learning the Job

While you are building working relationships with your staff, your boss, and your peers, you will also be learning the tasks that are part of your job. Even though you are an expert in some areas, or you would not have been given the job, you still need to learn these tasks from a manager's view. You will want to understand and learn all the details you may have missed as an employee or staff member. Now is the time to learn from your predecessor and your colleagues.

Your Predecessor

If you can meet with your predecessor, you will find that you can gather valuable information about your unit. Your predecessor can provide a unique view of the unit and provide insights into why the unit functions as it does. However, you will want to examine the information critically. You were hired to help the unit grow and improve. You will want to establish your own approach and style. Nonetheless, the information you receive can be useful if interpreted with careful judgment.

You may be facing a situation where you were brought in to make changes because your predecessor was not successful. In such a case, you may still want to meet with your predecessor, but recognize that the person may not be very objective about the organization.

If you can meet with your predecessor, plan the conversation to get to the information that will be most helpful to you. Subjects to raise include[8]

Department structure. Ask what works and what does not work about the current structure.

Mission and goals. Learn about your predecessor's view of the unit's mission and goals. How well is the unit meeting its goals?

Personnel strengths and challenges. Find out what personnel issues you will need to address. Learn how your predecessor views the staff. Then remember that you will want to make your own assessment.

Budget. Learn how the budget was developed. What is included and what is missing? What resources are needed for the unit?

Committee assignments. Are there particular committee meetings you should attend? How are decisions made? What is your likely role?

Hidden problems. Can your predecessor alert you to hidden land mines in the unit? What pitfalls do you need to avoid?

The information you gather in this conversation can be a helpful guide. But remember, your predecessor may have a hidden agenda. Be sure to weigh the information you get against other information you gather as you meet with your staff and colleagues.

Office Files

Another important source of information about the unit or department is the unit's operations manuals and files. These files may be online, and it is important to find out how to access electronic files and who can access these records or e-documents. From the written documentation, you will learn how tasks are supposed to be done. You can find out about policies and procedures, paperwork, and forms. While you will find that there are some variations in how tasks are actually done, the manuals will help you learn how the tasks should be done.

Reports. Annual reports, committee minutes, and task force reports are also a rich source of information. These historical documents will help you understand the origin and development of your unit. You will also learn what problems have been solved and which ones keep reappearing. If you cannot find reports for your unit, ask your staff if they have copies you could borrow. Check to see if your organization has an archive of historical documents and see if you can find unit reports there. Usually, someone will have copies of some of the reports you need. Do ask others for help in finding these documents.

Personnel files. The official personnel files will give you background information on each member of your unit. You will also see how staff have been evaluated, what problems have been addressed, and what successes have been celebrated. You may find it more effective to talk to each staff member first and begin to form your own judgments before reading past performance reviews. You will want to make sure you are being open and objective as you begin to learn about your staff. You will want to watch that you are not unduly influenced by your predecessor's view of the staff.

By reviewing the written documentation available about your unit, regardless of format, you will learn how tasks are done, how policies and procedures are carried out, and how the unit documentation is created and saved. All this information will help you learn your job as you learn about the group you now manage.

Summary

At the end of each of our new supervisors' first days, each sits down to take stock. Gina handled patron complaints, found out the budget was only slightly out of balance, and wondered what to do about the student who was not showing up for work. Gina realized that no one was going to create an orientation schedule for her or tell her how to do her job. Instead, Gina created her first major "to do" list and thought about how she should proceed with her job. Her list included a schedule for the next few months. On her list, Gina put the following:

Hold a brief fifteen-minute meeting each morning with staff
to review the work for the day, as a way to decrease the
number of unexpected crises and events.

Schedule individual meetings with staff members. Do two
per day.

Set aside one to two hours each day to read files, documents, and reports.

Schedule a meeting with her boss.

Schedule meetings with other supervisors. Try for one or two a week.

Review department goals and objectives and assess progress each month.

Tony also sits down to review his day. He calmed down a staff member who was upset about potential changes in workflow. He met with a few of his librarians and learned that their opinions on issues were very diverse. Learning to collaborate and work more as a team will be a key to the unit's success. Tony also decided to have coffee with Gina soon to compare notes as new supervisors. Tony's "to do" list included

Schedule thirty-minute meetings with each librarian and staff member in the unit.

Schedule twenty minutes each day, at a minimum, to read reports.

Schedule a meeting with his boss.

Have coffee with Gina.

By developing plans for learning about their unit and their jobs, Gina and Tony will be better able to manage their units even as they learn how to be managers.

NOTES

1. Elizabeth Fuseler Avery, Terry Dahlin, and Deborah Carver, *Staff Development: A Practical Guide,* 3rd ed. (Chicago: American Library Association, 2001).
2. Morey Stettner, *Skills for New Managers* (New York: McGraw-Hill, 2000), 15–27.
3. Peter Hernon, Joan Giesecke, and Camila Alire, *Academic Librarians as Emotionally Intelligent Leaders* (Westport, CT: Libraries Unlimited, 2008), 2.
4. Avery, Dahlin, and Carver, *Staff Development,* 65.
5. Robert Lefton and Jerome Loeb, *Why Can't We Get Anything Done around Here?* (New York: McGraw-Hill, 2004), 100–121.
6. Linda Hill, *Becoming a Manager* (Boston: Harvard Business School Press, 2003), 52.
7. Martin Broadwell and Carol Broadwell Dietrich, *New Supervisor: How to Thrive in Your First Year as a Manager* (Cambridge, MA: Perseus Books, 1998), 27–29.
8. Edward Betof and Frederic Harwood, *Just Promoted! How to Survive and Thrive in Your First 12 Months as a Manager* (New York: McGraw-Hill, 1992), 22–23.

Communication Skills

GOOD COMMUNICATION SKILLS are the key to being a successful supervisor because first and foremost, communication is about establishing and maintaining relationships. As a supervisor, you are responsible for building your team, establishing a good working relationship with your peers, and developing a positive relationship with your boss. Good communication skills are essential to developing these diverse relationships.

Good communication is about efficiently transmitting your message. How you communicate will set the tone for your unit. If you are clear in your communications, you will create a healthy environment. If you are abrupt and noisy, you will create a stressful environment. If you are always vague and unclear in your messages, you will set a tone of secrecy and uneasiness.

At the most basic level, communication involves a message, a sender of the message, a receiver for the message, and feedback about the transmission. (See figure 3.1.) Communication can be spoken (live and in person, recorded on a voice mail) or written (formal memo, handwritten note, e-mail, text message, IM, etc.), and it may include a nonverbal component (your physical "presence" in meetings with staff). Regardless of the method or medium, when communication is successful, information is "processed, reviewed, clarified, and revised until both the sender and receiver completely understand each other."[1]

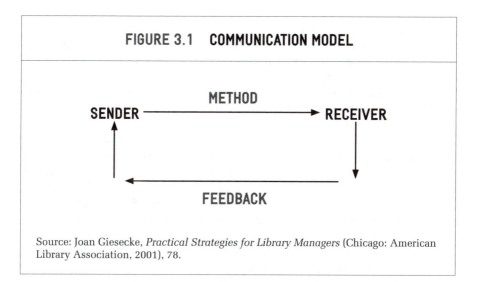

FIGURE 3.1   COMMUNICATION MODEL

Source: Joan Giesecke, *Practical Strategies for Library Managers* (Chicago: American Library Association, 2001), 78.

Know Your Audience

With whom do you want to communicate and why? Is the receiver your supervisor, a colleague, someone you supervise, or an external client (a library board member, an upset library patron, a colleague at another library, etc.)? What is the purpose of your message? Do you want to convey to staff a new personnel policy, a request for input on a possible new service, or an announcement of an upcoming meeting? The transmission method and message form will vary depending on what information you need to convey, whether an action or response is necessary, and how quickly action must take place. Our backgrounds, experiences, and personalities affect how we seek and use information. In effective communication, you will want to match the form of the message to the recipient's view of the world. Carl Jung identified four types of people: thinkers who are analytical and work with facts; intuitors who deal in ideas and concepts; sensors who are action-oriented; and feelers who are ruled by emotions.[2] Each of the personality types will hear a given message differently. Sharing lots of ideas with a person who prefers facts and figures will not be very effective. Talking in terms of feelings and values to a person who wants to do something and needs action will also be ineffective. Instead, frame your ideas in data for the thinkers in your unit and in action terms for the sensors. You can then effectively convey the same information to very different recipients.

Other factors, such as the message recipient's age, rank in the library relative to your rank, cultural background, and technological expertise and experience levels, may have a place in both how you deliver a message and how well it is received. Depending on the situation and the people involved, a supervisor may want to use more than one method to communicate the same message to different people.

Emergency communication. Gina's town is hit with a major snowstorm on a Friday evening and the mayor orders all city operations closed until Monday. The library director phones Gina and other supervisors on Friday evening to alert all of them that the library will be closed. Gina immediately contacts weekend staffers, including part-time high school and college student library clerks. She telephones one staffer at home, reaches the Sunday supervisor at his cell phone number, and sends text messages to the part-time clerks. Once she has reached all staff working the weekend shifts, she sends an e-mail message to the departmental e-mail alias, alerting everyone to the details: why the library closed, plans for reopening, where to find updates to the weather situation, and how to handle time cards for scheduled personnel.

Gina manages to reach all affected staff—through the medium most likely to reach them. By having a communication or contact tree in place prior to the weather emergency, she is able to share the news quickly and efficiently, informing those who need to know immediately and providing more detailed information for everyone as well.

New personnel policy on schedule adjustments. Tony's library administration wants to implement a new policy for scheduling. Tony's department has had a long history of flexible scheduling, or "flextime," and he is concerned about staff reactions. He himself had a flexible schedule before he became a supervisor. This is a big change for Tony's unit, and Tony decides that he will need to meet individually with the staff members most affected by the change as soon as possible so that he can answer any questions they may have about their specific situations. Then he will communicate with the entire unit at a staff meeting, or, if the timeliness of the announcement is a concern, he will send a detailed e-mail.

As a manager, Tony balances his responsibilities to implement the new policy with his care for his employees, taking the time to meet with staff individually to alert them to the upcoming changes.

Listening

After planning your message, you can then think about how you will listen for feedback. Active listening skills are crucial for supervisors. Obviously, you want to practice good listening skills when you are the message receiver. First, demonstrate that you are receptive to the message you are about to receive. Acknowledge the sender by nodding, injecting an occasional comment such as "yes" or "interesting" or "I see." Stay focused on the speaker and the message.

Show interest by listening carefully and attentively. Notice the speaker's emotions as well as the text of the message. Notice if the words match the emotions. If these do not match, take time to ask questions and clarify meaning until you understand how the speaker's emotional state merges with the message.

Be sure you are listening to the speaker rather than framing your response. It can be easy for a busy supervisor, with many demands on his time and many tasks to accomplish, to become distracted by other thoughts and not listen carefully. You need to be sure you understand the message before you respond. If you do not listen to and clarify the message being sent before you respond, you may find yourself responding to the wrong message. You will complicate the communication process when you do not practice active listening skills.

Try, as the receiver of a message, not to make judgments until you have received all the information that the speaker wants to communicate. Try to listen for understanding rather than listening only for agreement. Be open to hearing other ideas even when the ideas are different from yours. If you rush to a judgment or conclusion, you may miss important details or nuances in the message. You may then respond inappropriately and may unnecessarily complicate the communication process.

One way to force yourself to pause before you respond is to silently count off a few seconds before beginning to speak. This brief silence will ensure that the speaker has completely finished her thoughts and is not just pausing between points.

Once it is your turn to speak, begin by asking clarifying questions. Also, be sure to briefly summarize the speaker's key points before you frame your response. Only then can you be sure you accurately heard the speaker's message.

As the sender of a message, you also want to practice active listening. Be sure you hear your receiver's response. Watch for comprehension and understanding. Ask supporting questions and provide additional information if you sense that your message is not being received. By taking time to clarify the major points of your message and taking time to actively listen to responses, you will have a better chance of creating a successful communication encounter.

Reading

One communication challenge for supervisors is to keep up with all the written material and reading that are part of the job. This material can be in print or electronically delivered. Developing an efficient system for handling the reading of materials can make the job much easier.[3] Effective reading means developing a system for quickly scanning material, assessing the importance of the item, and locating the key messages. Keeping print material from accumulating into huge piles and finding a system to organize e-materials will help keep you from becoming overwhelmed. Sort items into categories ranging from urgent items you need to read and act upon immediately, to the items you want to read and study in depth, to those you can declare nonessential. For unimportant items, scan them quickly and move on. Delete them, send them to be filed, throw them out, or route them as needed, but do get them off your desk and computer. Act upon or write your response to urgent items as quickly as possible. You want to resolve these issues and keep them moving. For important, in-depth items, set aside time to concentrate on these issues and read the appropriate material. Find a time during your day or week that you can set aside for in-depth study. Use that time to thoroughly read and study the important items that have reached your desk.

By staying on top of your daily mail, paper, and e-mail, responding to urgent items, and taking time to study the truly important material, you can be sure you are not missing key messages in your organization. You will set a good tone for your unit, as issues will not become bogged down because you did not take time to keep up with your mail and e-mail.

Written Communication

As a supervisor, you will find that you need good written communication skills. You will be responsible for preparing reports, writing evaluations of your staff, developing policy statements, and communicating with your supervisors. In addition, in today's world of e-mail communication, you will also be writing information to your staff that traditionally may have been communicated orally.

Good writing takes practice.[4] Think about the message you want to convey and how you want that message to be delivered. Are you preparing a formal report to be shared with those above you in the organization? Are you sending a procedural change notification to your department? Are you communicating with groups outside of your organization? Each audience is different and has different needs. You want to be sure that your writing style is appropriate for the audience. For example, an academic-style report may be appropriate for a professional journal article but may not be effective for conveying information to your unit. A library-use policy may need two versions, one for print on paper and another for the library's website; the content will be the same, but the arrangement on the paper and screen may need to vary in order to effectively communicate with the two different audiences. An informal, chatty memo to your group may be fine to alert them to a minor change in policy. This same style, though, is not appropriate for your annual report. Be sure, then, that your style of writing fits with your audience and with the purpose of your communication.

Next, in preparing to write, you should review or outline the purpose of your communication. What do you want to accomplish with your writing? Do you want to entice the public to a program or convey a policy change? Both actions are important but have very different purposes.

Third, consider the message you want to relay. What are the facts you want to get across to others? What are the key points you want to be sure your audience recognizes in your writing?

Once you have identified your audience, sufficiently outlined your purpose, and decided your main message, you are ready to begin drafting your piece. Your draft may go through many versions before it is ready. Writing requires effort and editing. It is rare that a person can sit down and compose a memo or a report without needing to make changes and edit the document. Think about the order in which you convey the information. Your primary and important points should appear first. The readers should not have to guess at what you want them to remember. Put the most important message first. Then add in your next most important items, and so on until you have included all the points you wish to make. Finally, write a concluding paragraph or section to summarize your key points and close your piece.

Now comes the hard part. You need to review your work and edit the piece to make it as clear as possible. Some word-processing software packages have tools that can help with this, but human review is still necessary. Eliminate any extraneous and unnecessary words. Do not use five words if three will do. Use active sentence structures to maintain clarity.

Check for grammar. Do all your nouns and verbs agree with each other? Have you started a paragraph each time you have a new thought or idea to express? Do you have long sentences that cannot be easily understood? Look at how you can shorten and revise your work to increase clarity and understanding while still conveying all the points that you wish to make.

One helpful hint is to read your writing out loud. How does it sound? Do the words flow easily? Are the ideas clear? Reading your work out loud can help you catch grammatical errors, as well as noting when you have used more words than you need.

Good written communication is a core skill for supervisors. Taking your time and reviewing your work before you distribute it will help you become an effective writer.

E-mail

Some dangers in the world of communication involve the misuse of and mistakes made through e-mail communication.[5] It is too easy, sometimes, to think you can just sit down and compose an e-mail and fire it off without review. Poorly written e-mail messages can be as dangerous for a supervisor as a poorly written report. With e-mail, as with all communication, be sure you practice good etiquette. Be careful with your use of abbreviations. For example, not everyone knows instant messaging abbreviations that dominate some e-mails. Be sure you explain the abbreviations you do include.

Be thoughtful about when you use e-mail. It makes very little sense to send someone an e-mail message when you are sitting next to the person and can simply turn and talk to him. E-mail should not be used as a way to avoid oral communication. You will also want to be careful about who you send e-mails to and how you reply to messages sent to you. Do not copy everyone imaginable on an e-mail message unless the information is truly needed by everyone in the organization or group. Do not reply to all on a discussion list message if you are sending a private reply to the sender. Not everyone on the list wants to know about your lunch plans. Keep your business e-mails business-oriented and do not confuse business and social communication.

One other trap to avoid with e-mail is the tendency to send out an e-mail reply when you are upset or angry. That is not the time to be sending messages, even to close friends, as the message could be forwarded to others. E-mail is not a secure communication channel. Rather, treat it as you would a postcard and assume everyone around will be able to see the message. A list of practices to avoid in your e-mails is provided in figure 3.2.

Dangers of e-mail "reply all." The library board decides to postpone the annual fund-raiser this year due to staff shortages. Tony's unit typically organizes and staffs the fund-raiser, so he lets his unit know and he sends an e-mail to all library staff indicating that the fund-raiser will be postponed this year. A supervisor of another unit, who enjoys the fund-raiser himself and often receives input from patrons and staff about it, reacts angrily and responds to Tony's message questioning Tony's authority, accidentally copying to all staff. Tony feels undermined by his colleague; Tony's colleague is embarrassed by his e-mail gaffe and ultimately apologizes to Tony; staff members who had initially accepted that the postponement was necessary and unavoidable now experience lowered morale and wonder about the library supervisors' working relationship.

E-mail can be very effective when used correctly. E-mail is an efficient communication medium and can help you inform everyone in a group at the same time about a change. It can also help you document that you have relayed needed information to your group. It can help you send updates and non-time-sensitive information to a large number of people.

As a supervisor, think about what you want to communicate with your writing and then pick the best way to get your ideas across to your audience. Whether you are composing an e-mail message, jotting down a list of bullet points you want to mention at a staff meeting, or writing a formal report, remember to think about your audience, review your purpose, and then outline your message. Finally, edit, edit, edit! A well-written and edited e-mail will help you send the kind of message you want to send

---

FIGURE 3.2   E-MAIL DON'TS

1. Don't write what you don't want others to know.
   Ask yourself: would I want my boss or my mom to read this message?
2. Don't e-mail just because it seems easier.
   An e-mail thread that includes more than three new messages isn't easier—just pick up the phone or visit in person with your coworker.
3. Don't forget to use the spell-check.
   E-mail at work is still business communication!
4. Don't leave them guessing.
   Address your e-mails to the person by name and close with your name.
5. Don't make a bad impression.
   Send well-written, clear, and concise messages: grammar and spelling matter.
6. Don't forward unless necessary.
   Ask yourself: Should I summarize rather than forward? And don't forward without approval of the original sender (coming back to #1 above).
7. Don't overload attachments.
   Make it easy for your reader and their e-mail system.
8. Don't add personalized graphics.
   Back to #3: work e-mails are business communication.
9. Don't send flaming e-mails.
   Take care to not react emotionally. Consider drafting a response but then holding it for a while.

Source: "9 Things to Never Do in E-Mail" by Beverly Davenport Sypher, expert in business communication and associate provost for special initiatives at Purdue University.

---

to your group. A poorly written or repetitive report can just as easily hurt you. Communicating well is an art. Take time as a supervisor to practice the art of good writing each time you write.

Barriers to Communication

Unfortunately, noise in the environment can disrupt the transmission and receipt of the message. Noise can be any sort of disruption to your message. Noise can enter the communication system in a number of ways, including

Background chatter at meetings and side conversations can distract participants and prevent clear communication.

Interruptions can disrupt the speaker and cause the person to lose track of the message.

Too much detail can inhibit effective communication. The message can be lost when too many nonessential details are included.

Irrelevant messages cause noise in the system. Messages that are not relevant to the receiver are unlikely to be remembered.

Incomprehensible jargon can also confuse the message or lead to misunderstandings.

Badly timed messages can also be unproductive. For example, asking for a detailed report on a project just as someone is leaving for the day is not going to be helpful.

Personal prejudices, stereotyping, and biases can influence how one hears a message.

Confusing or conflicting body language can disrupt communication.

The emotional state of the sender or receiver can limit one's ability to send or receive information.

How can you minimize noise in your communication? Carefully planning your communication can make the difference between effective communication and noise pollution. Remember, "effective communication is primarily the speaker's responsibility."[6] Be sure you are being honest, open, and clear in your communication. You don't want the receiver of your message to have to read between the lines and guess at your meaning and intent. Be alert to signals from the receiver of the message that you are being unclear. Look for both verbal and nonverbal clues that can tell you if your message has been accurately received. Think about the purpose of your message and what you want to accomplish. Do you need someone to take action? If so, be sure you plan your message so that the action you want taken is clearly stated. Think about the recipients. How much information do they need? Is this an informed audience or one with limited knowledge of your subject? Plan your communication so you link the audience and the message. Be sure the subject of your message is clear and easily identified. Obscurity and ambiguity will only create confusion. Focus and clarity will help ensure that you get the results you want from your message.

Your Reputation Affects Communication

As a supervisor, you will find that your "reputation, credibility, and intention" impact how effective you can be as a communicator.[7] If you are viewed as an honest, straightforward supervisor who can be trusted, people are more likely to accept your communication at face value. They will not look for hidden meanings and devious messages. Rather, they will be open to communication from you and will try to understand what you are trying to say. If people see you as a supervisor who hides information, they will be more suspicious of communication from you. They will be more likely to look for hidden meanings and hidden agendas. Even when you are being open and honest, the staff may be leery of your communication and may be cautious in accepting information from you. As a supervisor, your actions will speak louder than words, to quote an old cliché. In communication, as in other areas of management, you will be successful if you think about what you want to accomplish, work with your staff to be clear about your intentions, and be open to communicating and receiving information.

Summary

General communication strategies. Good communication skills take practice to develop. Be sure you take time to learn to speak clearly, listen attentively, and respond appropriately.

Oral communication. Plan your communication carefully. Know what the key points are that you wish to convey. Limit how many points you make at any given time to the amount of information people can absorb. Providing more information than anyone can possibly comprehend in one session is not going to help you communicate your ideas.

Speak clearly and distinctly. Pause frequently and ask for questions to be sure your listeners are following your points.

Summarize your key points or actions to be taken to be sure your listeners remember the points you want to convey.

Practice active listening skills by paying attention to the speaker, clarifying the message before you speak, and taking time to be sure the speaker has finished before you begin to respond.

Written communication. If you are unsure about your writing skills, then take time to learn to write by writing. Practice your writing skills every day. Read other people's reports and analyze the writing style. What aspects of the report are clear to you? Are there sections that do not make sense? By analyzing others' writing, you can begin to identify what makes writing successful and what does not.

As you practice writing, use the following rules to help simplify your writing style.

1. Talk about it first. Know what you want to say before you start to write.

2. Talk to the reader on paper. Pretend the recipient of your letter is sitting across the table from you. Write your report or letter as if you were talking to this person.

3. Write to express, not impress. Write for understanding. Do not use long sentences when shorter sentences will do. Do not use so many big words that your audience cannot follow your meaning.

4. Short is better. Write enough to be clear and then stop.

5. Say it first and last. Put your purpose in your first sentence and summarize it in your last sentence.

6. Read for meaning, not glory. Reread your writing from the reader's point of view. Be sure your audience will understand your message rather than worrying about how to make yourself look good.

7. Don't strive for perfection. There is no such thing as the perfect report. Once your piece is understandable and well organized, let it go. You have other things to do besides reediting every single document you produce.[8]

Good communication skills come with practice. Good communication skills help you create positive working relationships with your staff, your peers, and your supervisor and will help lead to success in your role as a library supervisor.

NOTES

1. William A. Salmon, *The New Supervisor's Survival Manual* (New York: AMACOM, 1999), 93.
2. Arthur Young, *Manager's Handbook* (New York: Crown, 1986), 135.
3. Ibid., 138.
4. Ibid., 136–37.
5. Gary McClain and Deborah S. Romaine, *The Everything Managing People Book* (Avon, MA: Adams Media, 2002), 165–66.
6. Salmon, *New Supervisor's Survival Manual,* 97.
7. Ibid.
8. Young, *Manager's Handbook,* 143; and McClain and Romaine, *Everything Managing People Book,* 164–65.

4

Work Climate and the Art of Motivation

AS A SUPERVISOR, you are primarily responsible for the climate in your unit. You may not realize that you have great influence over how your staff will view the unit and the organization. If you are positive and inclusive in your approach, you can create an environment where employees feel the organization cares about them. If you see the organization in "us vs. them" terms, your unit will see enemies throughout the organization. If you are passionate about the mission of the organization, you can create an atmosphere of excitement that keeps your unit motivated, even in tough times.

One challenge you face in creating a good climate, though, is to learn to recognize what kind of environment exists in your unit and organization and to learn how to improve the environment if it is not as positive as you would like it to be. There are many ways to describe organization climates. In this chapter, we will look at two approaches to describing the climate in your unit and we will examine ways to improve that climate.

Character of the Organization

One way to describe the climate in an organization is to look at the character of the organization. How can you describe an organization in terms of character? William Bridges, in his book *The Character of Organizations,* presents a system for using the Myers-Briggs Type Indicator (MBTI) as a way to look at the character of an organization and the type of climate that character type creates.[1] His system gives supervisors a different way to think about the unit and about how to develop the unit to be successful.

To follow Bridges's view, it helps to understand how the Myers-Briggs Type Indicator system works for individuals.

> The Myers-Briggs Type Indicator is a four-letter personality-type designator created by Katharine C. Briggs and Isabel Briggs Myers in the 1940s from the theories of Carl Jung. The MBTI examines four aspects of our personalities and uses these to categorize sixteen possible personality types. The four scales, noted below, describe how people focus their attention, gather information, make decisions, and generally deal with the world.[2]

These four scales are then used to create the sixteen personality types: ENFJ, INFJ, ENTJ, INTJ, and so on.

Focusing Attention

E (extroversion)—relates more to the outer world of people

I (introversion)—relates more to the inner world of ideas

Gathering Information

S (sensing)—works with facts

N (intuition)—looks for possibilities and relationships

Making Decisions

T (thinking)—makes decisions based on impersonal analysis and logic

F (feeling)—makes decisions based on personal values

Lifestyle

J (judging)—prefers a planned, orderly life

P (perceiving)—prefers a flexible, spontaneous, open life

In the workplace, the sixteen personality types provide clues to how people will likely relate to work groups, decision making, and problem-solving activities. Understanding these relationships can help supervisors decipher the behavior of the staff.

William Bridges has taken the four broad categories behind the MBTI and created a way to look at the overall character of the unit. He looks at the organization's approach to its customers, how the organization gathers information and makes decisions, and how quickly the organization takes action. These four categories create a vocabulary for talking about the organization or unit.[3]

Focus or Orientation of the Unit

Extroversion—outward-looking organizations that look to the market to determine what direction to take

Introversion—inward-looking organizations that look to their own technical abilities and leaders' ideas to solve problems, set direction

Gathering Information

Sensing—look at facts, current realities, and details of a situation

Intuition—look at the big picture rather than the details

Making Decisions

Thinking—impersonal decision making, based on principles

Feeling—more value-driven decision making with a personal component

Dealing with the World

Judging—tend to make decisions quickly

Perceiving—tend to keep options open

Each of these characteristics will yield different climates and different ways of operating. Understanding the different orientations and approaches that work in the organization can help you build a successful unit.

How can you determine the character of your organization? Bridges includes a survey instrument in his book that you and your unit can take.[4] The results of the survey will help you identify the major characteristics of your organization. Once you have taken the survey, you will want to discuss the results with your unit. You should decide how well the results describe what you already know about the organization. You can also use these discussions as opportunities to talk about how you want to function as a unit, what strengths you want to highlight, and what challenges you face as a group working within the larger organization. As a supervisor, you may find that the conversations about the organization are more important than the results of the survey. By discussing how you want to operate as a unit, you will be better able to build a working climate that is successful for the unit and the organization.

How else can you use these ideas to your advantage? In addition to using the survey results as a way to begin a conversation about the unit, you can also use Bridges's approach to help you create successful proposals that are likely to be implemented. By knowing how to bring about change you can create a working environment that is geared to success. For example, if you and your unit wish to implement a new chat reference service or other new service, you will want to tailor your unit's proposal to match the characteristics of the organization. If your organization is basically an extroverted one that looks outward for ideas, then you will want to survey organizations that already have implemented the new reference service and describe their experiences in your proposal. If your organization is more introverted and inward-looking for advice, then you may want to ask the reference service experts in your organization to review your unit's proposal and help tailor your ideas to match the organization.

If your organization is more comfortable with facts and details, then be sure to include relevant facts and details in your proposal. For a chat reference service, include an analysis of the software used for the service, describe how reference shifts might be scheduled, and include details on the resources needed to implement the service. If, on the other hand, your organization concentrates on the big-picture idea, emphasize how chat reference fits into the overall service delivery program. Describe how the new service will enhance the work of the organization. While you still need to include details on the software to be used and how you propose to incorporate the new service into your existing structure, you will want to be more succinct and less detail-oriented in an intuitive organization than in a sensing organization.

By understanding the overall character of the organization, you can help your unit make sure that the work they do is presented in ways that will be successful in the organization. Your unit's ideas will be more likely to succeed. Your unit will be better able to contribute positively to the work of the organization. Members of your unit are less likely to become disillusioned with the organization when they can see their ideas having an impact on their work. Then you will have created a positive and successful climate for your unit.

Creating a Professional Environment

As a supervisor, you will also be responsible for creating and maintaining the professional environment of your unit. Your unit's success within the larger library organization will depend on the leadership you provide in this area. The first impressions we leave with library patrons, library board members, and our colleagues in other units are very important. Some libraries have policies in place, such as dress code or customer

---

FIGURE 4.1   PROFESSIONAL WORK ENVIRONMENT STATEMENT

The Professional Work Environment in University Libraries:

The University Libraries are a professional workplace, and it is important to maintain an appropriate work environment. Elements of that environment include interaction with patrons and professional appearance and behavior. Voices carry in the libraries in both the public and staff areas. Please be careful in what you say (refrain from using offensive language) and also be aware of how loudly you are talking.

While we do not have a formal dress code, please keep in mind that we are a business and need to present a professional appearance and environment. Appropriate attire means that skirts and shorts extend at or below fingertips and tops should not expose midriffs. Hats or caps should not be worn inside the building. Please refrain from wearing any clothing with offensive writing on it. Shoes are to be worn at work.

Source: University of Nebraska–Lincoln Libraries Policy, October 7, 2008.

---

service policies, which help manage these first impressions. If your library has a dress code policy, you should set a good example and help your staff to understand and follow the policy. If your library or larger organization does not have a formal dress code policy, you may want to consider adopting a policy for your unit. A sample policy is shown in figure 4.1.

Creating an Inclusive, Positive Climate

Another way to look at the organizational climate is to determine how inclusive the climate is for the diverse individuals in your unit. In an inclusive environment, differences among staff are recognized as strengths you can build on in the organization. Blending and integrating those strengths will create a positive working environment where staff are inspired to do their best work.

You can build an inclusive environment by building trust among the members of your unit, by treating everyone with respect, and by promoting good communication.

Trust. Trust develops when staff feel they are treated fairly and as individuals. In a unit with a high level of trust, rewards are the result of effort, not favoritism. Employees must know that if they perform at the required level, you will follow through with a reward that they value.[5] Staff must feel that their views are appreciated and their input is gathered and used. Office politics are kept to a minimum. Decision making is transparent, and staff can see the connection between input, decision making, and results.

Respect. Respect is another key element in creating a positive working environment. Again, when staff feel they are recognized as individuals, when their ideas are taken seriously, and when they feel their contributions are important, they will feel they are respected. If staff feel they are being treated as interchangeable parts, they may feel taken for granted and will not see the workplace as a positive environment.

Communication. Enough cannot be said about how important good communication is for creating a positive working environment. Good communication is a two-way process. In a positive environment, staff feel they are aware of what is going on in the unit and organization. They also feel their input is sought and used in making the unit a success. Feeling "in the know" is a major motivator to many staff and helps them understand how they can best contribute to the unit and organization. Staff want to be part of a successful organization. Good communication is a key part of helping staff know how they can contribute to, participate in, and benefit from working in the unit and organization.

Steps to Inclusion

What specifically, then, can you do as a supervisor to create a positive, inclusive working climate?

First, be sure you set the right tone for the office. You must understand and accept diversity in the unit and accept the diverse contributions each individual makes to the unit. You need to make sure you are not being disrespectful to staff members and that you do not tolerate disrespectful behavior from others. For example, do not tolerate inappropriate jokes or humor. Caution staff who make inappropriate remarks about others that they must stop. If the behavior does not stop, you need to take appropriate disciplinary action. Ignoring inappropriate behavior will create a negative environment for your unit and could result in legal action.

You need to share information with everyone in the unit and be sure individuals are not left out of the communication loop. You need to ask for input and use that input or explain why you cannot use input you received. In other words, make it clear to staff how you made a decision and how you used their ideas.

You also need to give credit to others for their work and ideas. You will quickly lose your staff's trust and respect if you take credit for and are rewarded for their ideas.

You need to practice listening to your staff. One of the hardest things to do as a supervisor is to really listen to ideas that run counter to what you believe and to try to find positive aspects in ideas that may not fit with your view of the unit. Even though it may be difficult to examine others' ideas, it is important to keep an open mind and explore alternative opinions. By doing so, you will see a broader view of an issue, explore new approaches, and expand your own understanding of an issue. By carefully listening to others and exploring views that do not match your own, you will help your staff members realize that their ideas are valued and therefore that they are valued as individuals and as part of the unit. For example, when talking with your unit about a new service, ask your staff for ideas and keep track of the many viewpoints expressed. Then summarize those ideas for the unit in order to let staff know that you heard and considered their ideas. Staff can express different viewpoints on scheduling desk shifts, for instance, from how long a shift should be to how many shifts each person should work. By sharing the diversity of viewpoints, the staff will know that they have been heard and will realize that there are many ways to set up the service. Understanding different points of view will make it more likely that staff will understand why all their ideas cannot be implemented.

When you can create an environment where staff are proud of what they do and feel a part of the mission of the organization, you will have the foundation for a very productive unit that can achieve excellence.

Individual Motivation

Once you have looked at the overall climate for your unit and at how you can make that climate as positive as possible, you will want to look at how to inspire each staff member to do the best he or she can do. As a supervisor, you are responsible for creating an environment where employees are motivated to do their best work. To succeed in creating a good working environment, you need to know what motivates your staff and how you can help them want to be productive.

Let us begin with a definition of the word *motivation. Motivation* can be defined as giving someone an incentive to act or giving someone a reason to do something. Motivation is also creating a feeling of enthusiasm or interest that makes someone want to do something. So the supervisor does not motivate someone but rather creates an incentive for action. Motivation itself is self-directed. Either a staff member will want to accomplish a task or he will not. As a supervisor, you want to create the best incentives you can to encourage staff to accomplish the work that needs to be done.

Theories of Motivation

What makes people want to act? Management theorists began to address this issue in the 1950s with the human relations school of management thought. Theorists looked at individual behavior and developed theories to explain why people act in certain ways. These theories identify for supervisors what factors they need to consider in creating a motivating work climate.

Before turning to the behavioral theorists, let us review the work of Douglas McGregor and his view of management styles and motivation.[6] McGregor defined two basic approaches to management known as Theory X and Theory Y. In Theory X, managers believe that most people do not want to work. Therefore, in order to have a productive workplace, supervisors must carefully monitor the work of the employees. Supervisors create detailed rules and procedures for staff to follow so that there is no uncertainty about what is expected or how the work is to be performed. Supervisors assume staff are lazy and will put forth the least amount of effort to get by. These supervisors create an environment that does not foster creativity, is very rule-bound, and in which staff have little or no say in how the work is performed. In Theory X, the motivating factor for staff is a paycheck. On the other hand, Theory Y managers believe people want to do a good job. These managers want to create a nurturing environment where staff can be creative and contribute to the organization. Employees in Theory Y want to be useful and productive. Their motivation is the reward of a job well done.

These two views of staff motivation create two very different workplaces. In Theory X, rules and procedures are crucial, and following the rules is the key to success. In Theory Y, staff involvement in the organization and participation in decision making lead to a productive environment. Theories X and Y illustrate how the principles of motivation that we follow impact the types of workplaces we create.

Two other major theorists in motivation are Abraham Maslow and Frederick Herzberg. Maslow looked at human behavior and theorized that people are driven by a hierarchy of needs.[7] First, people want to satisfy their need for food and shelter. Next, they will look for safety and security. Once these basic needs are fulfilled, people will try to satisfy their need for social affiliation or belonging to a group. Next, people look to fulfill their needs for self-esteem and to feel important and accepted as individuals. Finally, people have a need for self-actualization in which they seek continued growth and development. In Maslow's theory, people do not have to completely satisfy one need before moving on to the next. They may work on more than one need at a time. Still, unless the basic needs are fulfilled at a minimal level, people will not be thinking about higher-level needs such as group needs and individual accomplishment needs. For a supervisor, then, if staff cannot make ends meet on the salary they receive, they are first going to be motivated to find additional sources of income. Either they will change jobs or they will find a second job to provide adequate income to meet their needs for food, shelter, and safety.

Providing training so a person can learn about herself as an individual will not be effective if the person cannot meet her basic needs. Maslow helps you as a manager to recognize that the basic resources must be in place before managers can move on to meeting higher-level needs.

Frederick Herzberg took a different approach to motivation. He theorized that there are two basic sets of motivators: those factors that are positive motivators are called satisfiers, and those factors that are negative motivators are called dissatisfiers. Positive motivators include such things as recognition, the work itself, increasing levels of responsibility, and advancement opportunities. Dissatisfiers or negative motivators are factors such as salaries, policies, type of supervision, and working conditions. These negative factors can lead to poor motivation but they do not lead to positive actions. That is, these factors may make people leave an organization but they will not necessarily keep someone working in your organization.

While theories of motivation are useful and can help you as a supervisor understand why one way of motivating staff will not work for everyone, the theories do not necessarily offer practical suggestions for how to create an environment where staff are motivated to do their best. For that help, we turn to the Gallup Organization.

A third theory on motivation has been developed by the Gallup Organization and reported in the book *First, Break All the Rules*.[8] Gallup surveyed over one million individuals to identify those factors that separate organizations or units that are excellent performers from those that are only good.[9] They found that four factors can be used by managers to determine how to create an environment that is motivating to employees. These factors are

1. Basic resources to do the job

2. Individual needs

3. Social needs

4. Growth opportunities

Gallup isolated twelve questions that can be used to measure how well individuals believe that the organization is meeting their needs. These twelve questions can then be used to distinguish those environments that lead to high performance from those that do not.

The questions are rated on a scale from 1 to 5 where 5 is "strongly agree" and 1 is "strongly disagree." In excellent organizations, employees will answer "five" to all of the questions. The twelve questions are

1. I know what is expected from me at work.

2. I have the equipment and materials I need.

3. I have the opportunity to do what I do best each day.

4. Someone at work cares about me as a person.

5. In the last seven days, I have received praise for doing good work.

6. Someone at work encourages my development.

7. The mission or purpose of the company makes me feel my job is important.

8. My fellow employees are committed to doing quality work.

9. At work, my opinion seems to count.

10. I have a best friend at work.

11. In the last six months, someone has talked to me about my progress.

12. In the last year, I have had the opportunity at work to learn and to grow.[10]

These questions identify factors that are similar to Maslow's hierarchy of needs. However, the order for the questions is slightly different. According to Gallup, employees first want to know what they can get from the organization. The first two questions will indicate if employees' basic needs are being met. They are the organizational equivalent of safety and security needs.

Next, employees want to know what they can give to the organization, and questions 3 through 6 look at these factors. These are equivalent to Maslow's individual needs.

Third, employees will want to figure out if they belong in the organization, and questions 7 through 10 examine this issue. Here is where we find Maslow's social needs.

Finally, employees want to know if they can grow in the position, and the last two questions look at this point. Here are Maslow's self-actualization needs. Gallup has found that by reversing Maslow's individual and social needs, they are better able to identify excellence in the organization. The motivational theories of Maslow, Herzberg, and the Gallup Organization are compared in figure 4.2.

Motivational Factors and the Workplace

Gallup's questions provide a very practical way for managers to look at the environment they are creating in the workplace and examine what they need to do to move their unit to excellence.

FIGURE 4.2   THEORIES OF MOTIVATION

Maslow's Hierarchy of Needs	Herzberg's Concept	Organizational Focus	Gallup's Questions Hierarchy	Organizational Focus
Safety and security	Dissatisfiers	Basic requirements	Expectations and resources (Q 1–2)	Basic requirements
Social needs	Satisfiers	Contribute to the organization	Individual and self-esteem (Q 3–6)	Individual success
Individual needs	Satisfiers	Individual success	Unit focus (Q 7–10)	Contribute to the organization
Self-actualization	Satisfiers	Growth	Growth questions (Q 11–12)	Growth

Clarifying Expectations and Providing Resources

Managers should first be sure that they have been clear about their expectations. Have you met with each employee and reviewed the expectations for his or her position? Are the expectations included in job descriptions and performance evaluations? Employees should not have to guess what is expected of them. The supervisor should be able to clarify this information for each position.

Supervisors are also responsible for ensuring that employees have the resources they need to do their jobs. Staff find it very hard to be motivated when basic equipment and supplies are not available. Employees with inadequate equipment will underperform and will lose interest in the organization. No matter how many incentives a manager creates for her employees, if employees are scrambling to find supplies and resources, they will not be spending time improving performance.

Identifying Individual Needs

Once the basics are in place, supervisors should talk to each employee about what the employee feels she does best and how that can be a part of her position or tasks. If someone's talents do not fit the job very well, that employee may be in the wrong position. While she may be a good performer, she will not achieve excellence when she cannot do what she does best. Employees also want to know that someone cares about them and that they receive recognition for their work. Acknowledging good performance, encouraging staff, and letting staff know you are concerned about them as individuals will go a long way to creating a motivating environment.

As you are discussing each person's individual talents and ambitions, you will want to identify specific factors that help the person feel motivated to do a good job. Standard motivators include the following: a sense of achievement, a sense of power, a sense of belonging, and a sense of independence. As you talk to your staff, find out which of these needs are most important to them.[11]

To determine if the person is motivated by achievement, see if the person is goal-driven. Does the person like to work on projects? Is learning new skills important to him? If so, the person is likely to be looking for ways to be productive and reach new goals. Give this person new challenges. Include both short-term and long-term goals so the person can see that he is accomplishing tasks as a long-term project develops.

A person who likes to exert influence and attract attention is likely to be motivated by feeling in control and feeling powerful. These staff can be a challenge when they seek center stage and try to dominate conversations. Enable these staff to contribute positively to the organization by helping them to become in-house experts. Channel their energy into projects where they can express their opinions and be seen as important members of the group.

For staff who need to feel a sense of belonging, you will want to be sure the person has numerous opportunities to interact with colleagues. This person does not necessarily work well alone. Instead, find projects that require a group effort. These staff may also be the social organizers for the unit. Let them plan group events, staff luncheons, and other social opportunities. They will enjoy the opportunity to work with others and provide a positive social environment for the unit.

To determine if a person is motivated by independence, see if she questions procedures and policies that limit the individual's ability to decide how to carry out a task. You will want to be careful not to micromanage these staff. Instead, find ways they can determine their own way of achieving agreed-upon results. Of course, you will want to guard against giving the person so much freedom that the person does not follow important rules, ignores legal requirements, or refuses to work cooperatively with others.

Contributing to the Organization

After examining how to meet individual needs, it is time to look at how each person can contribute to the organization. Help employees see how the mission of the organization relates to their individual tasks. Talk to people about how they make a difference. Explain to the staff or students who shelve books how they make it possible for fellow patrons or students to more easily find materials when they take time to shelve materials correctly. Show cataloging staff how the work they do makes it possible for patrons to more easily identify needed materials. Each job in the organization is important, and as a supervisor you should be able to show how each position helps the organization reach its goals.

Supervisors should also be sure they are listening to staff and asking for input as appropriate. Staff will often have the best ideas on how to improve workflow and work procedures. As supervisors, we cannot be afraid to learn from our employees. Listening to staff is also a way that a supervisor can show respect for the employee. Reading or answering e-mail while listening to staff ideas will signal to the person that you do not care. When staff feel that you do not care about them as individuals, they will be less motivated to contribute to the organization.

Growing in Your Job

Finally, help people grow in their jobs. Staff do want to learn and to be challenged to improve. Motivated staff will seek out opportunities to try new things, to enhance their own skills, and to improve in their positions. As a supervisor, you can encourage such activities and reward people for their successes. Supervisors should talk to their staff about the progress they are making. Gallup has found that having a progress conversation at least once every six months will help staff know how they are doing. These people will stay motivated to excel.

When you have created a positive working climate, you will have a motivated staff that are inspired to do their best. Creating that climate, though, will take work as you learn how to successfully address the needs of the individuals in your unit while understanding the overall organizational environment. When you can match individual needs with organizational goals, you will have a motivated staff. When you ignore individual differences and try to impose one supervisory approach on all your employees, you will leave some of your staff unmotivated and uninspired. Although it takes time to find the right combination of strategies for each person, the time will be well spent, as you will be rewarded with a well-functioning unit. You will have staff who want to work and who want to make the unit successful.

Summary

Motivation comes from within individuals. You cannot motivate someone to work. You can, however, create an environment where staff are self-motivated to succeed.

Begin by analyzing the overall climate and character of your organization. Determine what strategies will be most successful within the overall climate of the organization.

Once you understand the overall climate of the organization, analyze the climate in your unit. Look for ways to create an inclusive climate that capitalizes on each person's strengths.

Determine the best way to create a motivating climate for each member of your staff. Talk to your staff about their needs. Adjust your style to address the needs of each person. Of course, you need to be sure that you are working within the overall character of the organization.

Regardless of which motivational theory you follow, or what set of advice you prefer, you will be most successful when you truly listen to your staff, understand each person's needs, and match each person's needs with the tasks and projects within the unit.

NOTES

1. William Bridges, *The Character of Organizations* (Palo Alto, CA: Consulting Psychologists, 1992), 2.
2. Kent Hendrickson and Joan R. Giesecke, "Myers-Briggs Type Indicator Profile and the Organization," *Library Administration and Management* 8, no. 4 (Fall 1994): 218–19.
3. Bridges, *Character of Organizations,* 2–3.
4. Ibid., 115–19.
5. Patricia Buhler, *Alpha Teach Yourself Management Skills in 24 Hours* (Indianapolis: Alpha Books, 2001), 166.
6. Ibid., 162–63.
7. Joan Giesecke, *Practical Strategies for Library Managers* (Chicago: American Library Association, 2001), 44–46.
8. Marcus Buckingham and Curt Coffman, *First, Break All the Rules* (New York: Simon and Schuster, 1999).
9. Ibid., 11.
10. Ibid., 43–45.
11. Morey Stettner, *Skills for New Managers* (New York: McGraw-Hill, 2000), 74.

Teamwork and Group Dynamics

MANAGING TEAMS IS part of the new challenge for today's managers. Interdivisional teams, horizontal work groups, and a variety of collaborative arrangements are replacing many of the traditional functional and hierarchical structures in our organizations. Managers today must manage interdependent groups and create a culture of cooperation in the midst of older management structures that emphasize and reward individual effort over group effort. How can managers bring these opposing processes together to create effective working groups?

Definition of Team

One of the first problems in determining how to manage groups is to figure out what type of working group or team environment exists or is desired in the organization. The term *team* is used to describe everything from tightly knit, interdependent working groups to loosely structured gatherings of individuals who barely work together. *Team* can refer to a unit or department, a group of managers, a two-person pairing such as a partnership, or the whole organization. Sometimes it seems that organizations have created teams simply by taking the departmental structure and renaming the departments as teams without making any changes in how the group functions or is managed.

Even in sports, it is difficult to identify a single type of team. For example, a football team is a highly structured group with defined roles. Players come to each other's aid only as prescribed by the structure and rules of the game. That is, the quarterback of the football team is not going to be on the field with the defense no matter how badly the defense is playing. Nonetheless, the group plays as a team, with individual roles subordinate to the team as a whole. Contrast this tightly knit, hierarchical approach to a golf team where individual performance is most important and there is little interdependence among the players. Baseball falls somewhere between these two types of teams, with players functioning independently in their individual positions but needing to interact in prescribed ways on the field if they are to win the game. In organizations, the independent golf team approach where each person does his own job with little interaction with others is becoming obsolete. Rather, organizations are finding that teams or work groups that require collaboration, commitment, and trust are more common and more productive than independent groups. But given this wide range of types of teams, what does the term really mean in the workplace?

Jon Katzenbach and Douglas Smith, in their book *The Wisdom of Teams,* provide a succinct definition of a team. They describe a true working team as "a small number of people with complementary skills who are committed to a common purpose, performance goals, and approach for which they hold themselves mutually accountable."[1] The key concepts in this definition help define the requirements for a true working team. To be a team, the group needs to be small enough that people can interact regularly and effectively. Team members get to know each other, build working relationships, and meet regularly. When the group gets too big, often beyond twenty-five people, it becomes more difficult to meet, to interact, and to work together. In larger groups, subgroups may form and the whole unit no longer functions as a coordinated team. Rather, the larger group may follow team values but not have the interactions that characterize effective teams.

Team members possess complementary skills rather than identical skills. Each team member brings unique skills to the group so that the group as a whole has all the proficiencies needed to accomplish assigned tasks. Having a group of people all with the same skills doing the same task is a working unit rather than a team. A group of online cataloging staff who all do the same task of cataloging materials using records on OCLC is a working unit, not a team. Each person's performance is independent of the others in the group. While group goals can be developed in a working unit, the individual employees can set their own pace and can do much of their work without consulting others as long as standards and expectations are clear. Here team values may be useful, but the group is not a true team.

The overall picture for a team is an interdependent group with a common goal or purpose. The team members are working toward and accept an agreed-upon purpose or set of goals. Individuals do not set their own goals. Rather, group goals define the course for the team. In football, for example, the defense may have team goals on how many turnovers they want to cause in a game. In the library, the interlibrary loan staff may create goals on the turnaround time and fill rate for requests. To achieve these goals, the group members must work together. Goals cannot be achieved by individual effort alone.

Team members also agree on how the work will be done. Internal procedures are explored and agreed to by the team. Problem-solving and decision-making processes are clear and understood by all members of the team. Team members also understand that each person contributes to the work of the whole. The amount of work that is done is equitably distributed, with each team member contributing to the best of his or her ability. Unlike groups where some people may contribute very little but get credit for the work of the whole, in a true team all team members agree to participate to make the team a success.

This brings us to shared accountability, a key factor in a true team. Team members agree to take responsibility for their own work and the work of the team. They help each other out as needed. They encourage each other to do the best that each member can do for the team. Individual responsibility gives way to group responsibility, mutual respect, and support.

Characteristics of Effective Teams

If the group you are managing fits the definition of a true work team, then your next step as a manager is to understand the characteristics of an effective team, because not all teams function well. Teams can be as dysfunctional as any unit or department in any management style. Successful teams, though, have the following characteristics:

Team members understand and support the organization's vision and goals.

Teams share a set of values about quality service.

Teams work to improve work processes and operations.

Team members discuss and agree as to how decisions will be made, how communication will occur, and how the group will be managed.

Team members listen to each other, respect each other, and trust each other.

Assignments and responsibilities are clear. Roles are clear and understood.

Teams effectively manage external policies, processes, and politics.

Teams set results-oriented goals.

Teamwork enhances the ability of the team members to work together; that is, team members continue to learn how to work together more effectively. Team members are satisfied to work together.

Teams adapt to changing environments, anticipate each other's moves, and learn to regenerate themselves as they work together.

Successful teams have committed, focused leaders who facilitate group success.[2]

Glenn Parker, in *Team Players and Team Work,* describes twelve characteristics of effective teams.[3] His list is similar to the list above. Parker includes clear purpose, informality within the team, participation, effective listening skills, civil disagreement, consensus decision making, open communication, clear roles, shared leadership, effective external relations, style diversity, and self-assessment as core characteristics of teams. As you review these characteristics of teams, as team leader, you will likely find that when the team members practice effective listening skills and open communication, the team will function as a coherent group.

Teamwork, then, can be described as a "frame of mind, a belief, and a commitment, not just a program."[4] In a team, group goals are more important than individual goals. Team members believe in the value of group processes and work to ensure that processes complement productivity. In other words, decision-making systems, communication systems, and work processes are equally important to meeting the team's goals. Productivity is not sacrificed to ensure good group interactions, nor are good group interaction skills ignored in order to maintain or improve productivity. A cohesive approach that brings team values together with team productivity is crucial if one is to create a true team.

How Can You Recognize a True Team?

An example from an interlibrary loan unit might illustrate some of the differences between a work group and a team. Imagine an interlibrary loan unit with five staff members and one supervisor. Two staff work on lending requests, two work on borrowing requests, and one serves as a reception desk attendant. A problem arises with the workflow between a branch library and the main library for obtaining books requested by other libraries in a timely manner. In a work group, the lending staff might discuss the problem with the unit supervisor and generate possible solutions. The unit supervisor might set up a meeting with branch and interlibrary loan staff. Then the group discusses the problem and proposes solutions. The supervisor decides which solution to implement. While the various staff involved provide input and discuss the issues, they are not empowered to make a decision and implement that decision.

In a team environment, the five interlibrary loan staff and the supervisor would discuss the problem with the branch staff. The group as a whole would generate options, assess possibilities, and decide the best way to improve workflow to meet agreed-upon goals for turnaround time. Lending and borrowing staff would participate in the discussion because changes in work routines could potentially impact the unit in any number of ways. By working together, the unit and branch staff will likely find solutions that work for all units involved. The group is not only responsible for implementing the changes but also accountable for their success.

Agreed-upon goals, responsibility, and shared accountability are all part of a true team environment. This still leaves the question of how to recognize a true team. What distinguishes a team from a working group? Again, we can turn to Katzenbach and Smith, who created a performance curve for teams and groups to illustrate the differences among types of working groups. They use performance impact and team effectiveness to distinguish between types of work groups.[5] At one end of the scale are working groups. Working groups are probably the most common form of structure in our organizations. In these units, individual effort is the primary measurement for unit success. Members may come together to share information, insights, or ideas on how to improve the unit. However, individual performance goals are more important than joint work products. Members of the unit interact but are not dependent on each other for either their own or the unit's success.

The second type of unit can be described as a pseudo-team. Here the work of the unit lends itself to true group-based performance, but the members of the unit do not and are not interested in working together to achieve unitwide goals. These units are not very productive because individual interests are more important to members than group success. Pseudo-teams may form when a manager or library director decides to rename work units as teams without making any changes in group interactions. The label for the group changes without any change in how the group functions.

The next type of group on the performance continuum is the potential team. Potential teams are those groups that are trying to improve group performance, are becoming committed to group goals, and are beginning to recognize the need for mutual respect and accountability. If you are a manager with a potential team, you can help the group achieve high productivity through team development and training. Potential teams in our organization offer managers the chance to implement change and achieve success.

Real teams, the next group on the continuum, are those units that meet the definition of a team and are reaching mutually agreed-upon goals. These groups are effective, productive, and can be successful over time.

High-performance teams are at the end of the continuum. These are groups that not only function effectively but also are deeply committed to each other's growth and success. These teams surpass goals, have high energy levels, and provide support for each other while meeting organizational goals.

The performance characteristics of these five types of groups are summarized in figure 5.1.

As a supervisor or team leader in a team-based organization, you will want to move your group from a potential team to a real or a high-performance team. If you have a work group, then a team structure may not be the best way to organize your unit. Here you need to look at the purpose and organizational goals for your unit. If interdependence is not a key factor in accomplishing your goals, then a team structure may not be

FIGURE 5.1   TEAM PERFORMANCE CHARACTERISTICS

Type of Group	Motivation to Perform	Measures of Team Success
Work group	Individual goals	Successful or not successful
Pseudo-team	Selfish interests	Not successful
Potential team	Organization sets group goals	Partially successful
Real team	Mutually agreed-upon goals	Successful
High-performance team	Surpass goals, committed to team growth	Most successful

needed. A solid working group that shares team values and meets its performance goals may be most effective for your unit. If you have a pseudo-team, you will need to do a lot of staff development and training to change your unit from a group to a team.

Developing Teams

Before you begin a team-building program, it is helpful to look at the context in which your unit operates because the context impacts team effectiveness. James Shank, in his book *Working in Teams,* outlines five factors that impact teams: environmental influences, goals, roles, processes, and relationships.[6] Let's look at each of these factors as they apply to our interlibrary loan unit.

Environmental influences. Environmental influences are the external forces that impact teamwork. These include such things as policies, reward systems, organization structures, customers, and governmental regulations. For the interlibrary loan unit, organizational policies such as who can use the service, how the service is funded, and what hours the library is open will frame how the unit functions. Reward structures for how salaries are distributed or what types of awards are available can also impact the unit. For example, if only individual effort is rewarded, it will be more difficult to convince the staff to work as a team. Lending operations staff may be less inclined to support borrowing staff if the former's efforts are not acknowledged by the organization.

Goals. Agreed-upon goals are the foundation for teamwork. Goals need to be clear, specific, and shared. In interlibrary loan, goals on turnaround time, fill rate, and quantity of work to be accomplished all determine how the group will design the workflow. For example, if a goal of twenty-four-hour turnaround time on lending requests is set and lending staff have an unusually busy day, then in a team approach, borrowing staff would help the lending staff complete their work. The team as a whole takes responsibility for achieving the goal.

Roles. Quite simply, clarifying roles means deciding who does what. For interlibrary loan, for example, the group needs to know who processes lending requests, who monitors OCLC requests, who oversees mail operations, and who manages the reception desk. It is also important for the group to know who the primary backup is for each task and how team members will know when their help is needed.

Processes. The term *processes* refers to the internal procedures that determine how the team does its work. In interlibrary loan, the group decides how long to spend on difficult requests before referring them to someone else. The team also needs to decide how decisions will be made and how meetings will be run. The team members decide and agree to which libraries will be contacted for materials and in what order, how consortium arrangements impact lending response and borrowing options, and how materials will be delivered to patrons. All these processes should be clear to all members of the team.

Relationships. The last factor to consider in understanding your team is the quality of the interpersonal interactions. Team members should develop their own guidelines on how they will interact, how difficult issues will be discussed, and how disagreements will be handled. In interlibrary loan, disagreements on what steps to take to resolve a patron problem need to be addressed. Staff must develop ways to express and address different opinions and viewpoints. If they do not address these issues, team effectiveness will suffer.

To summarize, these five factors are key considerations as you design team-building programs for your team. Addressing these areas in your development program will help improve team effectiveness.

Designing the Team-Building Program

Team-building programs can vary from a short discussion on the value of teams to a multiday retreat with a trained facilitator. How you design your team-building program will depend on how your organization functions and how the organization supports staff development. Does your organization have a formal staff development program or training unit? Does the organization have funds you can use to hire a facilitator to help? Does the organization have trained facilitators you can consult as you think about staff development? Know what resources you can use and what support you can find before you decide on a particular program or approach.

No matter how you design staff development efforts for team building, there are some common guidelines for success that you can follow.[7]

Establish clear goals. Be specific about what you want your team building to accomplish. Do you need new goals, new standards, or a new structure? Clarifying your goals will help guide your planning.

Get input. Effective team building starts by getting team members to help design the program. Involving team members in the planning will help get "buy-in" for the program. Imposing a training program on the group will be less effective.

Model constructive behavior. Focus on behavior and performance in the training rather than on judging opinions or positions. Staff should learn the effect that different behaviors have on the unit and how appropriate behaviors can improve team performance.

Stay work-oriented. It is important to avoid team building that can become too emotional, with too much sharing of non-work-related information. Stay focused on projects and the responsibilities of the team. In interlibrary loan, training examples should be based on the processes of borrowing and lending materials and on document delivery rather than on the personal lives of the team members.

Allow time for change. Team building takes time. Change will happen, but it will not happen overnight. Team members need time to practice new skills, to try new processes, and to explore new ideas. Look for incremental progress and reward even small changes that are positive.

Assess development. Teams can conduct self-assessments throughout the development and training process so that the team can judge its own progress. Have the team members individually complete assessment tools and then discuss the results. Team members can use these discussions as opportunities to plan and guide future development efforts.

Assessment tools usually ask team members to rank how well the team is doing in

clarifying purpose

clarifying expectations

developing open communication systems

providing mutual support

developing conflict resolution skills

clarifying decision-making processes

encouraging risk taking

sharing leadership

sharing feedback[8]

Develop realistic expectations. Credibility and trust are easy to lose if you set expectations that cannot be met by the group. Expectations for training should address those factors that are within the group's control. For example, increasing understanding of each person's role, clarifying team goals, and improving conflict resolution skills are all factors that the team can control. Training in these areas will result in team improvement.

Utilize outside consultants. Finally, if possible, it can be very helpful to engage an outside trainer or facilitator to assist with team development. An outside person can help facilitate communication and remain objective more easily than someone from inside the team. Bringing in an outside person can help the team see new approaches and find new ways of working together.

Following these concepts will help you design effective training for your group no matter what training methods are used.

Team Training Plans

There are many ways to develop training plans and many methods that can be used. As a manager, you will want to match the training method to your team's needs.

Describing all the possible training options is beyond the scope of this work. You can find helpful examples of training methods in the third edition of *Staff Development: A Practical Guide* by Elizabeth Fuseler Avery, Terry Dahlin, and Deborah Carver.[9] In their book *Just Promoted!* Edward Betof and Frederic Harwood include a matrix you can use to evaluate the type of training that is needed and the methods that will be most successful.[10] In *Learn Library Management* by Bob Pymm and Damon Hickey, you will find two exercises and a case study that will help you build effective teams.[11] Designing good training programs takes time, thought, and resources. Your organization's staff development experts can be very helpful to you as you develop programs to build and strengthen your team.

When Teams Fail

What causes teams to fail? Why don't all work groups succeed as teams? The causes for failure are numerous because teams are often a paradox. Team leaders and teams balance

individual differences and collective identity

support with confrontation

management authority with team autonomy[12]

These conflicting ideas and concepts must be brought into harmony for teams to succeed.

Numerous forces are working against team success in the organization. Some of these forces include lack of respect, selfishness, backbiting, politics, blame, and decision-making dilemmas.[13] Immature approaches to the team by individual team members can defeat even the best team-building efforts.

Lack of respect. If team members do not have respect for each other or for the organization, it will be difficult if not impossible to turn the group into a team. It may be more productive to move people out of the group and get new members in order to build a viable team.

Selfishness. When staff members care more about what they can get as individuals than they do about the group, you will have problems building a team. Staff who argue over who gets a new pencil sharpener or mouse pad are not ready for team building. Here, as a supervisor, you need to step back and start with basic training in good group skills before you can begin team building.

Politics. If organizational politics are more important than the team, you have an immature group. Again, look for training options for basic skills to help staff move beyond an individual focus to thinking about the group goals.

Blame. If the group starts the conversation about a problem with "who is to blame," you have an immature group. An interlibrary loan staff, for example, that blames others for poor turnaround time instead of looking for a solution they can implement is not a well-functioning team. Blaming poor shelving, branch staff ineptitude, or poorly documented patron requests are all examples of immature group behavior.

Decision-making dilemmas. Another area where teams can experience difficulty is in decision making. Team leaders may find that team members spend an excessive amount of time discussing choices but then are unwilling to reach a decision. This process leaves the team leader making the decisions. Bob Frisch refers to this process as the dictator-by-default syndrome. Frisch explains that the problem arises because team members are trying to reach consensus but are using their individual preferences in the discussions.[14] Mathematicians and social theorists studying the decision-making problem have noted that three or more people trying to choose among more than three options will generate conflicting majorities for all of the possibilities. Thus, an impasse forms and the team leader is forced to make a decision, and that decision will satisfy only a small portion of the team. To avoid the decision-making dilemma, Frisch advises teams to use different tactics, such as evaluating the pros and cons of various options in order to keep the discussion more open on the possible options; examining assumptions about the options in order to be sure options are not being prematurely eliminated; brainstorming activities that are focused on real possibilities and that avoid nonsense options; and devising new options that combine the best features of existing options. These strategies help the team have an open discussion of options in order to reach better decisions.[15]

In all these cases, the culture of the group or the group members need to change before true team building can begin.

Supervisor's Role in Teams

By now you may be wondering what your role as a manager is in the team environment. Are you a team leader, a team member, or just one of the crowd? What role do you play in this type of organizational structure? As team leader you are responsible for the following tasks.[16]

Understand and be committed to the team concept. First, as a manager, you need to understand the team concept. If you play favorites or reward and promote individual achievement over group goals, you will undermine team efforts. If you are not committed to a team structure, you will not be effective as a team leader.

Select team members. As team leader, you are responsible for choosing the members of your team. Look for complementary skills so you can build a group of people with the variety and depth of skills you need for success.

Develop people skills. As a manager, you need to recognize and acknowledge team members' skill-building efforts. Even something as simple as saying "Good job" or "That's a good effort" will support people-building skills. Recognizing that different people want different types of recognition is important, too. Some people like public recognition; others prefer a personal letter. As a team leader, you need to understand your team members as individuals at the same time you promote group coordination and collaboration. Being responsive to and supportive of team members will help maximize individual performance and contribute to team success.

Facilitate information flow. Another major role for you as leader is to facilitate, support, and promote the flow of information. You bring in information from the rest of the organization. You facilitate the sharing of information about your unit with the organization. And you support the coordination of effort within the group through the sharing of information. As team leader, you are responsible for encouraging quieter team members to participate and to express their opinions while working with more forceful members to learn to listen to their colleagues.

Coordinate with your peers. As team leader, you are charged with working effectively with other team leaders to advance the goals of the organization. In interlibrary loan, for example, you may be working with an acquisition unit to be sure that heavily requested items are considered for purchase. You may coordinate searching activities with a reference unit. You may work with a cataloging unit to be sure the catalog records contain enough detail for your unit to use to verify ownership of a particular item. In each of these venues, you want to represent the goals and needs of your team while sharing the concerns of other units with your group.

Pay attention to first meetings. As team leader, you will set the tone for how the group initially interacts. If you show that you are flexible, committed to team goals, and responsive to the group, you will set a positive tone that will carry the group through its first few meetings. By sending a clear signal that you support the team as a team, you will encourage the development of good team guidelines and processes.

Set clear rules for behavior. Help the group establish clear ground rules as they begin to form as a group. Agreements on attendance, discussion options, confidentiality, meeting process, and other issues should be established early on in the process so the team can function effectively as a group while they build their skills to become a true team. Disagreements or resentments over simple items such as the time allowed for personal phone calls or the length of breaks can destroy team trust and make the group dysfunctional. A positive working environment that promotes true harmony within the team, without covering up tensions or disagreements, will lead to a productive team.

Spend lots of time together. As a leader, you need to spend time with your team. Absentee management will not work in a team environment. Delegating work to the group and then disappearing from the unit will not work. Team efforts require the group to work together. As team leader, you need to be a part of the group at the same time that you provide leadership and help set direction.

Provide positive feedback and constructive advice. As team leader, you are also responsible for providing feedback to the group. The team needs to know how they are performing as a group, how they are meeting goals, and how they are interacting. Effective leaders provide appropriate coaching, feedback, and advice even as they function as part of the team. (See the team evaluation tool in figure 5.2.)

Keep goals relevant. As team leader, you can help guide the group to ensure that agreed-upon goals and purpose mesh well with the overall goals of the organization. When teams are working on multiple goals, confusion can arise when goals appear to be in conflict. As team leader, you will need to watch for such situations and help coordinate or sort through team activities so that the team stays focused on the overall organizational objectives. Gina, as head of a reference unit, knows that her organization values customer service. She also knows that there are a variety of ways to measure customer service. She works with her team, then, to develop goals for limiting the number of patron complaints or increasing the number of patrons served. Matching unit goals to organizational goals is crucial if the team is to remain relevant to the organization.

Create opportunities for others. Team leaders cannot take all the desirable assignments, praise, or glory and expect to have a successful team. Rather, true team leaders share opportunities, plum assignments, and rewards with the team. Watching staff develop into successful team members is a reward to a true team leader.

Do real work. Team leaders are important members of the team. While the role of team leader means that you have responsibilities outside of the team, you also have real work responsibilities inside the team. A team leader in interlibrary loan will help with lending requests or borrowing requests when needed and not just sit around while team members struggle to complete a day's set of requests.

FIGURE 5.2   EVALUATING YOUR TEAM DEVELOPMENT **WEB**

RATING TEAM DEVELOPMENT
How do you feel about your team's progress? (Circle rating)

1. **Team's purpose**
   I'm uncertain — 1 2 3 4 5 — I'm clear

2. **Team membership**
   I'm out — 1 2 3 4 5 — I'm in

3. **Communications**
   Very guarded — 1 2 3 4 5 — Very open

4. **Team goals**
   Set from above — 1 2 3 4 5 — Emerged through team interaction

5. **Use of team members' skills**
   Poor use — 1 2 3 4 5 — Good use

6. **Support**
   Little help for individuals — 1 2 3 4 5 — High level of support for
   individuals

7. **Conflict**
   Difficult issues are avoided — 1 2 3 4 5 — Problems are discussed
   openly and directly

8. **Influence on decisions**
   By few members — 1 2 3 4 5 — By all members

9. **Risk taking**
   Not encouraged — 1 2 3 4 5 — Encouraged and supported

10. **Working on relationships with others**
    Little effort — 1 2 3 4 5 — High level of effort

11. **Distribution of leadership**
    Limited — 1 2 3 4 5 — Shared

12. **Useful feedback**
    Very little — 1 2 3 4 5 — Considerable

Source: Adapted with permission from Arnold Bateman, *Team Building: Developing a Productive Team* (Lincoln: University of Nebraska, 1990).

Summary

Successful teams do not happen by accident. Building successful teams involves planning and effort. As a supervisor, before you begin on a team-building effort, assess your unit's readiness to be a team. Be sure the work of the unit fits well in a team environment. Evaluate the strengths of your staff and analyze the skills your unit will need to succeed as a team. Then, if the work and environment match the team concept, begin discussing the change to a team approach with your staff. Work together to develop strategies to become a successful team. By working together, your unit can move to a true team environment and will be successful in this different approach to managing the work of the group.

NOTES

1. Jon Katzenbach and Douglas Smith, *The Wisdom of Teams* (Boston: Harvard Business School Press, 1993), 45.
2. Edward Betof and Frederic Harwood, *Just Promoted! How to Survive and Thrive in Your First 12 Months as a Manager* (New York: McGraw-Hill, 1992), 128.
3. Glenn Parker, *Team Players and Team Work: The New Competitive Business Strategy* (San Francisco: Jossey-Bass, 1990), 33.
4. Martin Broadwell and Carol Broadwell Dietrich, *New Supervisor: How to Thrive in Your First Year as a Manager* (Cambridge, MA: Perseus Books, 1998), 273.
5. Katzenbach and Smith, *Wisdom of Teams,* 90–99.
6. James Shank, *Working in Teams* (New York: AMACOM, 1982), 19–21.
7. Betof and Harwood, *Just Promoted!* 131–32.
8. Adapted from Arnold Bateman, *Team Building: Developing a Productive Team* (Lincoln: University of Nebraska, 1990).
9. Elizabeth Fuseler Avery, Terry Dahlin, and Deborah Carver, *Staff Development: A Practical Guide,* 3rd ed. (Chicago: American Library Association, 2001), 125–46.
10. Betof and Harwood, *Just Promoted!* 140–42.
11. Bob Pymm and Damon Hickey, *Learn Library Management,* 2nd ed. (Friendswood, TX: Total Recall, 2007), 107, 110, 111.
12. Linda Hill, *Becoming a Manager* (Boston: Harvard Business School Press, 2003), 297.
13. Broadwell and Dietrich, *New Supervisor,* 268–69.
14. Bob Frisch, "When Teams Can't Decide," *Harvard Business Review* (November 2008): 121.
15. Ibid., 124–26.
16. Katzenbach and Smith, *Wisdom of Teams,* 119–27; Broadwell and Dietrich, *New Supervisor,* 270–71.

6

Inclusiveness and Diversity

What Is Diversity?

Importance of Recognizing Strengths

Retention

Summary

> *The great organization must not only accommodate the fact that each employee is different, it must capitalize on these differences.*
>
> —Marcus Buckingham and Donald O. Clifton,
> *Now, Discover Your Strengths*

GINA IS IN her office when Maria comes in and closes the door. Maria is a newly hired Hispanic librarian who is working with the multicultural program. Maria is concerned that she is being asked to serve on numerous committees and feels that some committees are asking her to serve only because she is Hispanic. She is frustrated with her position, because if she accepts all these committee appointments she won't have time to work with others on important multicultural issues. Maria tells Gina that if she can't find a way to do the job she was hired to do, she will need to find a new position. Gina takes a moment to collect her thoughts. Gina is now faced with the problem of retaining an important member of her reference team and fulfilling the library's commitment to diversity. After a moment, Gina comes up with a plan.

She suggests that she and Maria review all the committee assignments and pick only those assignments that are core to Maria's job. She says that then they will review Maria's workload and set priorities for being able to complete her most important tasks. Maria doesn't look convinced that this is a good plan. She feels bad that she will be saying no to committees that need to benefit from diversity. She feels a strong obligation to represent Hispanic people in the library and the campus. Gina realizes she needs to keep Maria engaged with the external community in a more focused way to be more effective. Gina turns to Maria and suggests that in looking at committee assignments, they pick those where Maria can make the most difference as a Hispanic member of the community, and she asks Maria if it would help to meet with other Hispanics in the community to talk about how to balance committee assignments across the campus to ensure that Hispanic voices are heard.

What Is Diversity?

At the most basic level, diversity is the existence and recognition of differences. These differences may be differences of ethnicity, nationality, gender, age, physical disabilities, or sexual orientation. Janice Joplin and Catherine Daus state, "Diversity encompasses any characteristic used to differentiate one person from others."[1] Building on this definition, managing inclusiveness and diversity means taking advantage of the diversity in the workplace to build a stronger organization. When we value diversity, we can "solve problems using multiple perspectives, relate to customers in their native language and culture, [and] improve communication."[2]

Over the next fifty years, it is anticipated that the United States will experience a sharp rate of growth in ethnic minority (nonwhite) populations. By the year 2050, minorities will account for 50 percent of the overall U.S. population.[3] These changing demographics mean that unless the library workforce also experiences a significant increase in the hiring of minority library workers, librarians and library staff will increasingly be serving students, faculty, and citizens who are not like themselves. The recruitment and retention of a diverse workforce, while an important issue for libraries during the past few decades, is now more important than ever.

In this chapter we will discuss the benefits of a diverse workforce, challenges for supervisors, and how to recognize strengths and capitalize on differences in your employees.

The Diverse Workforce

A library (or any organization) with a diverse workforce, with individuals willing to share new ideas based on their backgrounds and experiences, will be in a better position to meet the needs of our changing user populations. Better problem solving and increased creativity and innovation are the results of well-managed diversity in an organization.[4] A culturally diverse library staff brings different perspectives to library work, which traditionally, at least in the United States, has had an Anglo-European cultural context. Many libraries have developed diversity plans to help guide their work in this area. Consult with your library administration to see if your library has such a plan.

As a supervisor, you have an important opportunity to help create a diverse unit, as well as a unit with staff members who have an appreciation of and respect for diversity. Your unit will move forward to meet organization goals more fully by promoting acceptance of and respect for different people, ideas, and opinions. Recognizing differences in learning styles and communication styles will enable you to work most effectively with staff members you supervise.

Cultural Differences

Mainstream American culture has been heavily influenced by white/Anglo cultural norms. Creating an environment that welcomes, values, and respects all members requires developing an understanding of cultural differences and a realization that not all members of a particular culture will exhibit the same traits or behaviors. For example, researchers have studied variations in preferred learning styles for Native Americans, Hispanic Americans, African Americans, Asian Americans, and European Americans. As a supervisor, you will want to consider learning style preferences when you are training new employees and providing development opportunities for current staff.

Gender Differences

Even though we have made strides in achieving gender equity, understanding gender differences, without stereotyping employees, is still important today. Libraries traditionally employ more females than males, although upper-level management positions in libraries continue to include a disproportionate number of males. Gender differences may account for many of the communication issues that arise in libraries. Compounded by generational differences and cultural differences, gender differences may have major implications for supervisors.

Men and women bring different strengths to the workplace. Gender-based differences in approaches to communication, problem solving, and relationships are evident in young children and continue throughout our lives.

Boys tend to play in hierarchical groups with one boy acting as leader, giving orders, and telling others what to do. Boys play games with winners and losers and elaborate systems of rules. In contrast, girls play in small social groups that are inclusive within the group. Their games do not necessarily have winners and losers. Girls are more concerned with being liked than with attaining status within the group.[5]

In the workplace, this playground behavior pattern continues. Generally, men are more likely to be directive, to tell others what to do, to resent interruptions, and to value completion of tasks and goals. Women tend to work at a steady pace, not consider interruptions as a problem, prefer face-to-face or group interaction over written, impersonal communication, and maintain a complex set of relationships. Men seem to be more task-focused, while women are more relationship-focused.[6]

These generalizations may help you as a supervisor understand or interpret behavior that is different from your own. But as a manager, you will want to be sure you are not seeing your employees as categories or stereotypes. Use the research that helps explain gender differences to understand how to adapt your style to be more effective. You want to capitalize on each person's strengths, not discount someone based on an arbitrary category.

Gina manages a reference department of six reference librarians. She wants the group to function well together, but she recognizes that much of their work is done as individuals in reference transactions (on the reference desk or an online chat reference service, as well as in individual sessions with library users). Her department has three men and three women in it. The previous reference manager, Gina's predecessor, often seemed to apply gender stereotypes in the department. He usually asked the women to arrange all departmental social functions and to pitch in when others were on leave. Gina needs to be sure she takes care to expect the same level of cooperation from all employees, regardless of gender.

Gina will also want to consider how she communicates. She will need to balance her approach, being direct and directive when appropriate and using a more inclusive language style as well.

Gina can do a lot to promote harmony in the unit by recognizing different approaches and styles and using those differences to bring multiple perspectives to the unit's work.

Physical Disabilities

In your role as supervisor, you are responsible for working with your library or organization to provide a welcoming and inclusive environment for all staff, including those with physical disabilities. For staff who are deaf or hard of hearing, always face the staff member when speaking with him. This will help the staff member to hear as much as possible and allow him to see lip-reading cues. Consider carefully the seating arrangement in the work area and at meetings. Provide written material prior to meetings or presentations so that the staff member has some time to process information. For visually impaired staff, be sure that written documentation is clear, black-on-white copy. Policies and procedures should be conveyed verbally to the employee. During meetings and presentations, be sure that seating is available to allow the staff member to hear as much as possible. When feasible, tape-record meetings so that the staff member can review them as needed. If mobility is an issue for a staff member, work with the employee to determine appropriate tools and work space configuration. If arm or hand mobility is limited, consider structuring job duties so that the staff member works together with another staff member for tasks that require lifting, and so on. When speaking with a staff member in a wheelchair, sit down during your discussion so that you are both at the same eye level. Do not make assumptions about wheelchair users; lower body mobility may be their only difficulty. In this case, they are no different from any other staff person who is seated. Look for areas where your library or organization can improve access for individuals with physical disabilities.

Sexual Orientation

Gay, lesbian, bisexual, and transgendered (GLBT) staff members seek a safe working environment where all employees are treated with respect, regardless of their sexual orientation or identity. As supervisor, you can set the tone for your department or unit by your responses to GLBT issues. Respond to negative remarks or jokes in a way that demonstrates that you, and the library, do not tolerate this sort of disrespectful behavior. Other staff will respond to the way you handle these situations. Educate yourself about GLBT issues if you are not already familiar with them. Learn more about local resources on campus or in your community; many campuses have GLBT offices that can provide information and assistance.

Importance of Recognizing Strengths

Recognizing the strengths of your individual staff members can help you to channel their activities in the way that will be most beneficial to your unit. There are a number of personality indicators or traits surveys to help individuals determine their areas of strength. As with all surveys or testing measures, their findings should be considered as just a small part of the package that individuals bring to their positions and should never be used to stereotype employees. As Gordon Lawrence states, "We tend to stereotype those who are most different from ourselves because we understand them less well—a rule that holds true for type differences as well as cultural, racial, etc."[7] As a supervisor, it is your responsibility to ensure that if your organization does use personality-type indicators, you work with staff members in your unit to examine their own stereotypes and not impose them on their coworkers.

Two common workplace personality measures are the Myers-Briggs Type Indicator (MBTI) and the Gallup StrengthsFinder Profile.

MBTI

As stated previously, the Myers-Briggs Type Indicator is a personality-type designator created by Katharine C. Briggs and Isabel Briggs Myers in the 1940s based on the theories of the psychologist Carl Jung. The MBTI examines four aspects of personality: attention focus, information gathering, decision-making style, and lifestyle. It uses these factors to categorize sixteen possible personality types. The sixteen types provide clues to how people will likely relate to work groups, decision making, and problem-solving activities. Understanding these relationships can help supervisors decipher the behavior of staff. In work situations, these factors can be described as follows.

FOCUSING ATTENTION

E (extroversion). Extroverts like variety and action. They can be impatient with long, slow jobs. They like having people around. They are interested in results, getting the job done, and how other people do it. Often extroverts act quickly, sometimes without thinking.

I (introversion). Introverts like quiet for concentration. They tend to be careful with details and dislike sweeping statements. They are interested in the idea behind their job. They dislike telephone intrusions and interruptions. Introverts like to think a lot before they act. They work contentedly alone.

GATHERING INFORMATION

S (sensing). Sensing types dislike new problems unless there are standard ways to solve them. They like an established way of doing things. They work more steadily, with realistic ideas of how long it will take. Sensing types usually reach a conclusion step-by-step. They are patient with routine details and impatient when the details get complicated.

N (intuition). Intuitives like solving new problems. They dislike doing the same thing repeatedly. They work in bursts of energy powered by enthusiasm, with slack periods in between. Intuitives reach a conclusion quickly. They are impatient with routine details and are patient with complicated situations.

MAKING DECISIONS

T (thinking). Thinking types do not show emotion readily and are often uncomfortable dealing with people's feelings. They may hurt people's feelings without knowing it. They like analysis and putting things into logical order. Thinkers need to be treated fairly.

F (feeling). Feeling types tend to be very aware of other people and their feelings. They enjoy pleasant people, even in unimportant things. They like harmony. Feeling types' efficiency may be badly disturbed by office feuds. They need occasional praise.

LIFESTYLE

J (judging). Judging types work best when they can plan their work and follow the plan. They like to get things settled and finished. Sometimes judging types may decide things too quickly. They want only the essentials needed to begin their work.

P (perceiving). Perceptive types adapt well to changing situations. They do not mind leaving things open for alterations. They may have trouble making decisions. Perceivers want to know all about a new job.

StrengthsFinder Profile

The Gallup Organization, over the course of many years of surveys and research, determined that the best managers have two assumptions about their staff: each person's talents are enduring and unique, and each person's greatest room for growth is in the areas of his or her greatest strengths.[8]

The Gallup Organization found thirty-four patterns, or themes, that are the most prevalent themes of human talent. The thirty-four themes are

achiever	developer	learner
activator	discipline	maximizer
adaptability	empathy	positivity
analytical	fairness	relator
arranger	focus	responsibility
belief	futuristic	restorative
command	harmony	self-assurance
communication	ideation	significance
competition	inclusiveness	strategic
connectedness	individualization	woo[9]
context	input	
deliberative	intellection	

These thirty-four themes are the basis of the StrengthsFinder Profile, introduced in the book *Now, Discover Your Strengths,* by Marcus Buckingham and Donald O. Clifton. The StrengthsFinder's purpose is to help individuals find the areas where they show the greatest potential for strength. For supervisors, recognizing areas of staff talent will enable them to help individual staff members make the most of their potential. Gallup calls this "individualization."[10] By focusing on each employee's individual strengths, you can adapt the way you work with the employee in areas such as your communication style, how you provide feedback, and how you motivate for optimal performance.[11]

Buckingham and Clifton provide suggestions for how to manage each of the themes or strengths of staff in *Now, Discover Your Strengths.* Once you know the top themes for an employee, you can work together with the employee to develop her strengths.

Retention

Retaining a diverse workforce is crucial. Building a culture that welcomes diverse opinions and experiences is the first step in retention. There are many ways to change an organization's culture. One way that some libraries have adopted is to become a learning organization. Learning organizations value sharing ideas throughout the organization. Members share experiences, skills, and expertise, and in doing so they build respect for all members of the organization and create an organizational culture and work environment of inclusiveness. This provides a strong foundation for retaining a diverse workforce.

Important aspects of retention include on-the-job training, opportunities for challenging work, opportunities for advancement, flexible scheduling, competitive compensation, and other monetary and nonmonetary rewards. With an increasingly diverse and changing workforce, supervisors face new challenges. Issues related to single-parent households, dual-career parents, sandwiched employees (i.e., those who are caring for their children as well as their own elderly parents), older workers, gay and lesbian employees, and individuals with commitments outside of work and family life are increasingly common dilemmas for human resources offices, employees, and supervisors.[12] Many libraries have made a commitment to providing staff with ongoing opportunities to develop the skills to function effectively in a diverse workplace. Check to see about training opportunities at your library or larger organization.

Summary

Today, diversity is much more than just affirmative action programs. Affirmative action, while providing a framework to ensure fairness in hiring, has limited influence regarding long-term organizational change. Successful supervisors in diverse organizations possess attributes and skills that are not necessarily of great importance in more traditional organizations. These attributes and skills, sometimes described as core competencies or key behaviors, will enable supervisors to effectively manage staff and to move units and departments forward. Continuing to operate as

FIGURE 6.1 DIVERSITY DOS, DON'TS, AND OTHER ADVICE

DOS
- Be sensitive to differences among people.
- Treat everyone with interest, compassion, and sincere concern.
- Encourage everyone to participate (be supportive, especially if they are shy).
- Solve tough problems privately.
- Hold all staff accountable for minority and equity issues.
- Admit we are all prejudiced about something and learn to overcome your own.
- Be willing to say, "If I show prejudices, let me know."
- Take all people seriously.
- If you are having a problem, don't ignore it, seek assistance. Ask colleagues or the equity office or equivalent for help.
- Become a multiculturally sensitive supervisor and encourage others to also be advocates.

DON'TS
- Don't use these differences to form or respond to stereotypes.
- Don't jump to conclusions based on stereotypes.
- Don't (or allow others to) stereotype or make jokes about people of color.
- Don't (or allow others to) stereotype or make jokes about women.
- Don't treat minority staff differently.
- Don't express amazement when minority staff or women do well.
- Don't be confrontational in public.
- Don't expect all African Americans or any ethnic group to have a particular accent or the same accent.
- Don't use minority or female examples just as extremes (i.e., always negatively).
- Don't single out minority staff to answer minority questions; the same goes for women.
- Don't use power to hide personal mistakes.

OTHER ADVICE
- Differences do exist among people.
- These differences do affect how individuals interact in the workplace.
- Be observant of interpersonal interactions.
- Cultivate the habit of noticing details of these interactions.
- Be especially observant about how you interact with your unit or department.
- Watch details such as eye contact and your pattern of involving staff.
- Create a context where people have names and distinct identities.

- Talk privately to staff who are always silent.
- Be careful about giving differential attention.
- Be extremely careful about casual remarks (especially those made quickly or stressfully).
- Learn to recognize your own racist and sexist language.
- Avoid racist and sexist language, correct others who use it, and ask that you be corrected.
- Seek out minority colleagues in your field for assistance.

Source: Adapted from "Thoughts on Diversity by UNL Faculty," a University of Nebraska–Lincoln internal document for campus faculty.

usual, without taking advantage of the opportunities that a diverse work-force offers, will result in a unit falling behind institutional initiatives.

As a supervisor, you must be prepared to work with a varied and diverse staff. You should be aware of your own opinions or biases and how they might influence your interactions with staff who have different values. Flexibility and creativity will be key in this regard. When you treat people as individuals with their own strengths and you value each person's strengths, you will be well on your way to creating a climate that encourages and respects diversity. Figure 6.1 gives some helpful advice when supervising a diverse workforce.

NOTES

1. Janice R. W. Joplin and Catherine S. Daus, "Challenges of Leading a Diverse Workforce," *Academy of Management Executive* 11, no. 3 (1997): 32–47.
2. Bob Rosner, *The Boss's Survival Guide* (New York: McGraw-Hill, 2001), 187.
3. Martha E. Bernal, ed., *Valuing Diversity in Faculty: A Guide* (Washington, DC: American Psychological Association, 1996).
4. Taylor Cox, *Creating the Multicultural Organization: A Strategy for Capturing the Power of Diversity* (San Francisco: Jossey-Bass, 2001), 6.
5. Deborah Tannen, *You Just Don't Understand: Women and Men in Conversation* (New York: Ballantine Books, 1990), 43–44.
6. Sally Helgesen, *The Female Advantage: Women's Ways of Leadership* (New York: Doubleday Books, 1990), 19–24.
7. Gordon Lawrence, *People Types and Tiger Stripes* (Gainesville, FL: Center for Applications of Psychological Type, 1996), 97.
8. Marcus Buckingham and Donald O. Clifton, *Now, Discover Your Strengths* (New York: Free Press, 2001), 8.
9. Ibid., 81.
10. Ibid., 171.
11. Ibid., 174.
12. Ellen Ernst Kossek and Sharon A. Lobel, eds., *Managing Diversity: Human Resource Strategies for Transforming the Workplace* (Cambridge, MA: Blackwell, 1996), 230.

7

Policies and the Legal Environment

U.S. Employment Laws

Avoiding Legal Quagmires

Summary

POLICIES AND PROCEDURES are the organization's way of defining roles and responsibilities. They set the boundaries for individual actions, defining how managers interact with the organization. Many of our policies are developed to address legal issues and to outline how the organization implements various laws and regulations.

As a manager, you need to be aware of the legal responsibilities you have and you need to know how your organization handles those legal issues. You will also want to know what assistance you can expect from the organization if you do have a problem and what liabilities you face as a manager. While you may be tempted to hide from legal issues and try to avoid conflicts that can result from different interpretations of policies and rules, as a manager you are legally responsible for responding to problem situations. Not acting on personnel issues, for example, can be as dangerous for you individually as taking the wrong action would be. For example, if you are aware of a case of alleged sexual harassment in your organization, even if it is not in your unit, and you do not report it, you could still be liable. Once you, as a manager, are aware of a problem, the organization is assumed to be aware of the problem. Failure to act can result in the employee winning a complaint or suit against the organization because you neglected to act.

Rather than running from your role as manager in order to avoid legal entanglements, you can significantly decrease the chances of problems going awry by following good personnel management practices. You can protect yourself as a supervisor when you create a collaborative working environment instead of a litigious environment.

U.S. Employment Laws

Employment laws are numerous and complex because there are a variety of federal laws, state laws, executive orders, and local laws and regulations regarding the selection of employees and the treatment of individuals in the workplace.[1] Some laws apply only when an organization reaches a certain number of employees, while others apply to all organizations. The laws and regulations in the employment area change as new laws are passed, as courts render decisions, and as regulations are rewritten. It is your responsibility to remain current on changes in employment laws. Work with your organization's personnel and legal departments to stay abreast of changes that impact your organization. If your organization does not have the support systems you need, seek assistance from county or state offices; local, state, or national library associations; and other business and professional associations that can help you. Not knowing the law is not a valid excuse for acting inappropriately or not acting at all.

Many employment laws and regulations seek to protect employees from discrimination and harassment. Numerous laws and regulations exist that define this important policy area and define fairness in the workplace. Many of the policies that organizations have relating to fairness started with the Civil Rights Act of 1964, which includes the concept of equal employment opportunity (EEO). The many guidelines surrounding EEO policies are meant to provide for equal opportunities for all without regard to race, religion, origin, or gender. Many organizations have also added sexual orientation to the list. EEO guidelines apply to hiring decisions, pay, promotion decisions, and firing decisions, as well as to how you manage the work within your unit. As a manager, you want to be sure that you are not discriminating against an individual because of that person's characteristics.

Another important law that you need to understand is the Fair Labor Standards Act passed in 1938, which outlines compensation issues, defines the forty-hour workweek, sets a minimum wage, overtime pay, and defines exempt and nonexempt employees. Exempt employees are those staff who are not covered by the requirements of the Fair Labor Standards Act. Exempt employees may meet the following guidelines.

They are salaried employees.

They have hire-and-fire authority.

They direct the work of others.

They make their own decisions about how to do job tasks.

They spend most of their time engaged in management duties.

Nonexempt employees are covered by the regulations of the Fair Labor Standards Act.

As a supervisor, be sure you are not asking nonexempt employees to work overtime unless they are compensated to do so. You will also want to be sure that employees correctly record time worked so that overtime is properly identified. It is not useful to have employees, for whatever reason, decide that they will simply work extra hours and not record the time. The organization is still responsible for ensuring that staff are appropriately paid. As the supervisor, you need to be sure that staff follow the rules so that the organization is not liable for violating the law.

The Equal Pay Act of 1963 also addresses the question of compensation and clarifies the concept of equal pay for equal work. This law prohibits an organization from paying women less than men for the same position and job tasks.

The Age Discrimination in Employment Act of 1967 makes it illegal for an organization to discriminate against people who are forty or over. As the workforce in libraries ages, and as staff postpone retirement, accusations of discrimination based on age could increase. Be sure you are not inadvertently discounting the contributions of older employees, stereotyping your staff, or withholding advancement opportunities from staff as they age.

The Occupational Safety and Health Act of 1970 sets standards for creating a safe and healthy working environment. As a supervisor, you have responsibilities for providing a safe working environment. This includes such issues as "ergonomic furniture, air quality and ventilation, placement of office machinery (photocopiers, printers, etc.), cabling."[2] While some of these issues may be handled by a central unit in the library, you still have responsibility for reviewing your own area for safety issues. Providing appropriate step stools, for example, for staff who shelve materials or need to reach materials from higher shelves is an example of providing a safe environment. Reminding staff not to stand on chairs to reach things is another example.

The Americans with Disabilities Act passed in 1990 protects staff with disabilities from discrimination. The definition of *disability* is fairly broad and covers a wide range of conditions. The act also established the concept of "reasonable accommodations" for individuals with disabilities. Employers are required to make reasonable accommodations for a "disabled" person who is qualified for the position, unless doing so causes undue hardship to the employer's business. The person does have to be able to perform the essential functions of the position. Therefore, it is very important that the job description for the position incorporates all of those essential functions. Be sure to keep up with changes in this area as case law develops and the boundaries of the act are clarified.

Another law important to understand is the Family and Medical Leave Act (FMLA). Passed in 1993, it provides for job-protected leave for family or medical reasons as defined in the act. The reasons for using family and medical leave (FML) include a serious health condition that makes an employee unable to perform his or her job duties; the need to care for a spouse, child, or parent who has a serious health condition; and the need to care for a child after birth, adoption, or foster care. Regulatory changes in 2009 for the FMLA added benefits to military personnel and refined the definition of the term *employer*. Check with your organization to find out when FML may be used and how the organization outlines the reasons for using FML as regulations in this area change. At a maximum, a person's position is protected for up to twelve weeks of FML per rolling calendar year. Leave may be with or without pay, depending on the organization's leave policies. Organizations need to have policies on how they implement FML, and you will want to be sure you understand how the law is handled in your organization.

You will want to carefully monitor changes in the laws in your state, county, or city that could impact your work as a supervisor. Some states have now passed anti–affirmative action laws that make it illegal for those in public institutions to discriminate against or grant preferential treatment to any person or group based on race, sex, ethnicity, or national origin.[3] Although you may hold any number of opinions about such laws, as a supervisor your responsibility is to be aware of how this type of initiative impacts the way you make decisions. For example, in public institutions, these laws may impact hiring processes. While you may still seek a diverse pool of qualified candidates for a vacancy, you will want to have objective, defensible criteria for how the hiring decision is made. Again, it is important that as a supervisor you keep track of local changes that impact your environment.

These laws address some of the common issues you face as a supervisor. They do not, however, cover everything you need to know as a manager. To find out more about which laws affect your work, consult with the human resources experts in your organization. Know when you should contact legal counsel for advice. Perhaps the best course of action as a manager is to remember that if you have any doubts about how to handle a personnel issue, ask for help rather than guess. Making a mistake or avoiding a legal issue can be disastrous to you and the organization. Asking for help and getting legal advice can save you time and decreases the chances that problems will escalate.

General Legal Issues Impacting Libraries

Personnel laws are not the only legal area that you need to monitor as a supervisor. In the library field, you should also be aware of and familiar with copyright laws, intellectual property laws, and electronic licensing issues. Of course, you should be knowledgeable about censorship issues, First Amendment rights, banned book issues, and equitable access to information, just to name a few areas that impact libraries. The American Library Association (ALA) website provides information about the political and legal issues impacting libraries. The Washington office of the ALA keeps track of legislation that may impact the field. Many websites exist that outline these various issues and provide guidelines for libraries addressing political and legal issues. If you are a supervisor in a department with both librarians and staff, be sure that your staff, as well as the librarians, are aware of the key issues that impact the unit.

Avoiding Legal Quagmires

One way to avoid legal quagmires is to create a positive working environment for your staff and to practice good personnel management. When employees know the organization's policies regarding the many aspects of employment law, and your staff know that you are consistently following those policies, you are less likely to have problems. Employees become concerned when they feel they are not being treated fairly. The challenge for you as a supervisor is to figure out what defines fair treatment within your unit and in your organization.

What Is Fair?

Definitions of the word *fair* include terms such as reasonable, unbiased, done properly, and free from self-interest or prejudice. Notice that being fair is not treating everyone the same. Nor is it treating everyone equally. Rather, fairness means treating people as individuals while following standards and policies. Fairness means that everyone has the opportunity to compete for positions, for rewards, and for advancement. It does not mean that everyone will advance. Staff will have the opportunity to apply for or seek new challenges. It does not mean that everyone will succeed.

To create a unit where staff feel they are treated fairly, the rules and guidelines for how decisions are made, how staff are evaluated, and how promotions are granted need to be clear and understandable. When staff understand the rules, they are more likely to understand how decisions are made and why they may or may not get a promotion or other rewards.

When guidelines are clear, it is easier to show that personnel decisions are made as objectively as possible. For example, if you are responsible for recommending merit salary increases, then staff should understand what factors are taken into account when making salary decisions. If the performance evaluation is the basis for increases, then it will be important to demonstrate how the evaluation scores translate into dollars or percentage increases. If you cannot explain how you made your recommendation on merit increases, then you will be creating an environment that will foster suspicion. You will not be seen as fair by your staff.

Discrimination

A perceived lack of fairness can result in accusations of discrimination or harassment. Discrimination and harassment are complex areas that you need to understand as a manager. You need to know your own biases and be sure you are not making decisions or taking actions based on them. While you may not be able to eliminate your own biases, you can understand them and can refrain from using a prejudiced view in the workplace.

Besides understanding yourself, as a manager you need to understand the complex legal perspective of discrimination and harassment. Again, know your organization's policies in this area. Be sure you are clear on how to recognize and respond to inappropriate behavior in the workplace. Failure to act on cases of discrimination or harassment could make you as liable as the person who is exhibiting the inappropriate behavior.[4]

To help create an environment where it is clear that discrimination and harassment will not be tolerated, you can do the following.

Act when you hear about behavior that makes you suspicious.

Talk to employees who may be involved in inappropriate actions or find out what has occurred.

Remind staff about organizational policies on workplace behavior.

Take appropriate action based on organizational policy and procedures.

Encourage staff to report incidents of inappropriate behavior. Help staff understand that reporting problems is not "tattling" on fellow workers but is protecting all members of the unit and organization from potential problems.

Investigate or report complaints that come to you, following organizational policies and procedures. Do not dismiss a complaint because you cannot imagine the staff member behaving inappropriately.

Do not tolerate inappropriate jokes and stories. Nothing in the workplace is "just kidding."[5]

Most important, document your actions. You will need the
written evidence as you pursue an investigation, and if
the organization is going to be able to take action, you will
need to show that the problem was handled appropriately.

Handling accusations of discrimination or harassment can be touchy.
You can be successful when you carefully follow your organization's policies, when you consult with the proper authorities, when you document
what you have done, and when you take time to carefully address the
problem. These problems will not go away. You must address them in
order to resolve them and to again create or re-create a positive working
environment.

Handling Complaints

Despite your best efforts to demonstrate fairness, staff members may still
feel that they are not receiving the same benefits as others in the unit.
Complaints may arise when someone in the unit receives a promotion,
a larger raise, or additional training opportunities. When you are faced
with a staff member questioning your actions, you can handle the situation most effectively by taking time to listen carefully to the staff member and by being prepared to explain your decision. The steps you take
will depend on how your organization handles any particular problem.
However, in any situation, you need to actively address the issue. This is
not the time to hide or to try to cover up a problem. The sooner the organization can address a problem, the more likely the issue will be successfully resolved.

What are some ways you can begin to address a concern? Imagine
you are deciding whom to promote in your unit. You have two possible
internal candidates, Sally and Jane. Based on qualifications, you choose
Sally. However, Jane believes she should get the promotion because she
has been in the unit longer. Jane accuses you of being unfair. What should
you do? When faced with an accusation of unfairness regarding a promotion decision, try the following techniques.

Plan ahead for potential questions by having a clear set of criteria
for personnel decisions. Make sure that job advertisements for promotion
opportunities outline the skills needed for the position and the qualifications that are sought.

Prepare for a conversation with an unhappy staff member by reviewing your notes about how you made your decision. This is not the time to
guess at what you did or to be vague about the process you used to make
a decision.

Focus on the staff member who has questioned the decision and
not on the person who received the promotion. Maintain confidential
information and do not reveal personal information about the successful

candidate. In other words, do not explain why the other person got the promotion.

Instead, explain what skills were needed and review the qualifications as noted in the announcement of the position. Then review the staff member's performance regarding those skills. This approach assumes you have documented any skills or performance issues in the annual performance review. This way you can refer to written documentation that the person has already seen to illustrate your points about skills.

Be direct and factual, yet sensitive to the person's feelings. Treat the staff member with respect.

Focus on the staff member's strengths and how she can improve her performance and develop the skills needed for other promotional opportunities. However, be very careful that you do not promise her that she will succeed the next time she applies for a promotion.

Discuss development plans and career goals with the staff member. Turn the conversation into an opportunity to help the person with career planning.

Do not expect the staff member to agree with your decision or to thank you for the conversation. Instead, give the person time to reflect on the conversation.

Follow up later with the staff member about ideas for career development. Help the staff member find ways to use her strengths to excel and therefore possibly qualify for rewards and advancement opportunities.

Fairness is all about helping staff to become the best employees they can become. If you are consistent in how you apply policies and rules, and are clear about your expectations for workplace behavior, you will go a long way toward creating an environment that helps staff feel they are respected and are being treated fairly.

Why Problems Develop

Problems can develop in an organization when the top management and the organization do not take time to generate and implement appropriate personnel policies and procedures. But procedures alone will not resolve problems. Once policies and procedures are in place, management must ensure that the following occur:[6]

Appropriate training. Inadequate training of supervisors increases the chances that supervisors will not respond appropriately to problems.

Following written agreements. Not adhering to written contracts and union agreements will result in problems for the manager and the organization.

Consistent enforcement of procedures. Policies and procedures apply to all members of the unit. Excusing poor performance by one person while expecting compliance by others will result in problems.

Clear understanding of fair treatment. Perceived unfairness will cause staff unrest and create problems for the unit and the manager.

As a supervisor, take time to learn about employment laws, policies, and regulations. Then follow the policies in a consistent manner. You will be more successful as a supervisor when you are perceived to be fair.

Summary

As a manager, you are responsible for knowing and following the organization's policies, particularly those that are based on employment laws. Employment laws change as current cases are decided, regulations are written, or legislative action occurs. Be sure you keep informed about changes that impact your workplace. Ignorance of the law is not an excuse for inappropriate actions. When in doubt, seek advice from your personnel office or legal counsel.

Your best defense as a supervisor is to be fair and to be consistent. Creating a good working environment where staff are productive and feel respected will go a long way toward eliminating potential legal problems.

NOTES
1. Gary McClain and Deborah S. Romaine, *The Everything Managing People Book* (Avon, MA: Adams Media, 2002), 204.
2. Bob Pymm and Damon Hickey, *Learn Library Management,* 2nd ed. (Friendswood, TX: Total Recall, 2007), 80.
3. Valerie Richardson, "Obama Helped Defeat Anti-Affirmative Action," *Washington Times,* November 8, 2008; www.washingtontimes.com/news/2008/nov/08/obama-helped-defeat-anti-affirmative-action.
4. McClain and Romaine, *Everything Managing People Book,* 211.
5. Ibid., 212.
6. Deryl Leaming, *Academic Leadership* (Boston: Anker, 1998), 111–12.

8

Hiring and Interviewing

Job Descriptions

Hiring Processes

Background Checks

Negotiating the Offer

Summary

GINA HAS JUST been given the task of heading a new three-person team in the university library to develop a program to help patrons search, create, and use image databases. Gina gets to hire two librarians to work on her team. Gina would like to call up a few friends from library school to work with her on this project, but she knows she cannot do that. Gina's organization requires that she do a national or regional search to find the best people for the job. Gina has never conducted a search before. What should she do? Gina asks the human resources staff for help.

Determining the work that needs to be accomplished and selecting employees to do that work are two of the most important responsibilities of a supervisory position. Whether you are filling an existing vacancy or are fortunate to have an entirely new position, consider carefully what sort of work you would like the incumbent to accomplish. Your library or larger organization very likely has guidelines for writing a job description, advertising a position, interviewing applicants, and making a hiring decision. Working within these guidelines, you will be able to interview and hire the best candidate for your position opening.

Job Descriptions

The hiring process begins with a good job description. Job descriptions include the basic functions of the position and serve a variety of purposes.

For supervisors, the job description provides a framework for staff performance evaluations. For the employee, the job description identifies the essential job functions and helps the employee to understand what is expected of him.

Job descriptions should include a job summary, a detailed list of duties and responsibilities, necessary qualifications, and, if pertinent, any physical requirements for the position. The listing of duties and responsibilities should be detailed enough that a new employee can understand the tasks to be accomplished. Many position descriptions include the percentage of time devoted to each task, as well as an indication of whether the task is essential to the position. The use of clear, concise, and consistent language is very important for delineating duties and responsibilities, particularly when a task may be done by more than one employee.[1]

For Gina, developing job descriptions for her new positions is a challenge. Still, she needs to outline the key tasks of the job and the qualifications that are needed. For these digital reference positions, Gina might ask for experience with image databases, experience with software packages, experience with creating websites, or experience on digitization projects. Because these are entry-level positions, Gina may put experience under "preferred qualifications" and seek people with a strong interest in technology instead of experience.

Hiring Processes

Libraries, like all employers, have requirements and guidelines for hiring related to federal employment and equal opportunity legislation. If you work in a large library, you may have a human resources person in the library. For some public libraries, the city government's human resources office may be the source for guidelines and regulations. For small college or university libraries, a central campus human resources office may handle personnel for all of the campus. Depending on the situation in your library, work with the appropriate human resources department to be sure that you are following all the necessary procedures.

Preparing for the Interview

Prior to interviewing a candidate, review the requirements of the job. Review the position description (which lists the specific tasks to be performed on the job, as well as the methods, techniques, technology, and tools or equipment used to accomplish these tasks). Make note of unusual working conditions and other specific demands of the job in order to adapt the interview to elicit relevant information.

Develop your interview questions well in advance and relate those questions to the requirements of the job. Even experienced supervisors may occasionally wonder about the appropriateness of asking particular questions. The best advice to follow is that if a question is not job-related, do not ask it. Questions about an applicant's name, address, age, race/color/national origin, gender, religion/creed, sexual orientation, citizenship, marital/parental/family status, military service, criminal record, or disability should not be asked unless they pertain to the job. For example, if you need to verify degree or past employment information, it is all right to ask whether an applicant's work records are under another name, for the purpose of accessing these records. However, you should not ask the ethnic origin of a name, if a woman is a Miss, Mrs., or Ms., or request a maiden name. Because diversity is such an important issue in today's libraries, and we want to convey this to our job applicants, it may be tempting to ask questions related to a candidate's ethnicity at interviews. It is permissible to state that your library is an equal opportunity employer. However, you should not ask anything that would require a candidate to indicate race, color, national origin, or gender. For additional examples of legal and illegal questions, see the quiz in figure 8.1.

FIGURE 8.1   LEGAL AND ILLEGAL QUESTIONS: A QUIZ

QUESTION: You are interviewing a woman for a position in your circulation department. She mentioned during the interview that she is a single parent. Because the position requires a weekend shift once each month, is it okay to ask, "Can you arrange for child care?"
ANSWER: NO. Even though she volunteered the information about having children, this question is not appropriate. However, you can ask if she is willing to work the required schedule.

QUESTION: You are interviewing a man for a position in your access services department. Because he is responsible for collecting money from photocopy machines, is it permissible to ask him, "Have you ever been arrested?"
ANSWER: NO. However, it is okay to ask him if he has ever been convicted of theft, because the crime is related to the position. Convictions, if related to the position, are pertinent. Arrests, however, are not.

QUESTION: You want to hire a cataloger for foreign-language materials and need to know what languages the applicant can read and at what level. Is it permissible to ask a question such as, "What languages do you read fluently?"
ANSWER: YES. This question is perfectly acceptable because the answer is relevant to the performance of the job.

Carefully review the application and résumé prior to the interview. Familiarity with the candidate's application paperwork, so that you do not have to refer to it often during the interview, will allow you to concentrate on asking questions and listening carefully to the candidate's answers.

During the Interview

The climate created in the interview is important. Create a welcoming atmosphere, away from noise and interruptions. Introduce yourself to the candidate. Determine the candidate's preferred name and refer to it during the interview. Set a tone for a friendly exchange of comments and allow communication to develop freely in order to build mutual confidence.[2]

Describe the job and the library. Keep in mind that an interview is a two-way process. The candidate needs to know about the position, your department, salary information, training opportunities, and other information that will help him or her make a decision about accepting the position if it is offered. You want to learn as much as possible about the candidate's qualifications for the position.

Asking applicants for examples from their past work history or educational experiences will reveal areas of knowledge, skills, and abilities required for them to be successful on the job. By the close of the interview, you want to have an accurate and balanced picture of the applicant's qualifications and job motivation. Behavioral, situational, and competency-based interview questions will provide the best information for determining if the applicant can do the job. If you have a formal set of core competencies for your library or unit, it will be important to ask interview questions that will be helpful in determining whether your applicant meets or could meet a level of competency in areas important to your unit. Regardless of whether you have formal competencies, you will most likely have a set of knowledge, skills, behaviors, and attributes (the components of formal core competencies lists) that are important for the particular position and important to your organization. To elicit information about candidates' knowledge, skills, behaviors, and attributes, you might ask the following questions.

If analytical skills or problem solving is a competency, examples of questions to consider asking include the following:

Walk me through a situation in which you had to get information by asking many questions of several people. How did you know what to ask?

Describe a time you had to ask questions and listen carefully to clarify the exact nature of an internal/external customer's problem.

If creativity is a competency, you might ask questions like this:

> Tell me about a way in which you worked with other staff to develop creative ideas to solve problems.
>
> Describe how you've gone about learning a new technical task.
>
> In your current position, what have you done differently than your predecessors?
>
> Tell me about a creative idea you had to improve a library service.
>
> Tell me about a unique approach you took to solve a problem.

If working in groups (teamwork) is important for the position, consider asking:

> Can you give me an example of a group decision you were involved in recently? What did you do to help the group reach the decision?
>
> Describe a time you worked with a group or team to determine project responsibilities. What was your role?

If you value flexibility and adaptability in employees in your unit, consider asking:

> Tell me about an important project/task/assignment you were working on in which the specifications changed. (What did you do? How did it affect you?)
>
> Tell me about a time you had to meet a scheduled deadline while your work was being continually interrupted. What caused you to have the most difficulty and why?
>
> Going from [position] to [position] must have been difficult. Tell me about a challenge that occurred when making that transition. (How did you handle it?)
>
> Describe a time you had to significantly modify work procedures to align with new strategic directives.

To determine leadership ability or potential, consider asking:

> Tell me about a time you inspired someone to work hard to do a good job.
>
> Describe a face-to-face meeting in which you had to lead or influence a very sensitive individual.

Tell me about a time you were able to convince someone from outside (your department, etc.) to cooperate with you on an important project.

What strategies have you used to communicate a major change to employees? Which strategies have worked and which have not?

Describe a situation in which you had to translate a broad or general plan into specific goals.

For positions where customer service is important, consider asking:

In your current job, how do you know if your internal/external customers are satisfied? (Give a specific example.)

Tell me about a time when you were able to respond to an internal/external customer's request in a shorter period of time than expected. Contrast that situation with a time you failed to meet an internal/external customer's expectations. (What was the difference?)

As a [position], how did you ensure that you were providing good service?

Sometimes it's necessary to work with a customer who has unusual requests. Please describe a time when you had to handle an unusual request that seemed unreasonable. What did you do?

Some days can be very busy with requests from customers and coworkers. Please describe a time recently when you didn't have enough time to completely satisfy a particular customer. How did you handle the situation?

If planning skills are critical to the position, consider asking:

Walk me through yesterday (or last week) and tell me how you planned the day's (or week's) activities.

What procedure have you used to keep track of items that need attention? Tell me about a time you used that procedure.

What objectives did you set for this year? (What steps have you taken to make sure that you're making progress on all of them?)

Sometimes deadlines don't allow the luxury of carefully considering all options before making a decision. Please

give an example of a time this happened to you. What was
the result of your decision?

Tell me about a time you were faced with conflicting priorities.
In scheduling your time, how did you determine what was
a priority?

To determine the applicant's level of technical knowledge or expertise,
consider asking:

Describe a project, situation, or assignment that challenged
your skills as a [position]. What did you do to effectively
manage the situation?

Sometimes complex projects require additional expertise.
Describe a situation in which you had to request help.

Have you ever had to orient a new employee on a technical task
or area? How did you do it?

Describe a time you solved a technical problem.

What equipment have you been trained to operate? How
proficient are you?

What word-processing packages can you use? How proficient
are you?

Give me an example of a project that demonstrates your
technical expertise in [web page development].

Describe how you've gone about learning a new technical task.

How much experience have you had operating a [mouse,
keyboard, word processor, etc.]?

Describe the most challenging work you've done.

To determine the level of a candidate's interpersonal skills, consider
asking:

Working with people from diverse backgrounds or cultures can
present specific challenges. Can you tell me about a time
you faced a challenge adapting to a person from a different
background or culture? (What happened? What did you
do? What was the result?)

Our relationships with coworkers are not always perfect. Tell
me about the most challenging relationship you had with
a coworker. Why was it challenging? What did you do to
try to make it work?[3]

In addition to the kinds of questions just outlined, Gina will want to ask specific questions about technology interest and skills. Gina may find that a candidate who is enthusiastic and willing to learn is a better fit for this new venture than someone with a lot of technical skills but poor interpersonal skills. In other words, hire talent and remember you can teach skills. Recruiting an enthusiastic learner can be more successful in the long run than someone who does not fit well in the organization and is not enthusiastic about the challenge of starting a new project.

During the interview, your job is to listen, ask follow-up questions when necessary, and evaluate the candidate's answers to try to predict future performance. Practice good communication skills, such as active listening, reflecting, and reframing, and you will learn much about the candidate.

If you find the candidate is giving short answers and you are not learning enough about the person, ask follow-up questions. Continue to probe the answers until you feel comfortable that you have learned all you need to from the candidate. Candidates can be quite nervous, particularly if they are new to the job market. You can help the person by asking questions that help her explain her skills and interests. Do not settle for a "yes" or "no" answer if you want more information. Ask again if needed. This is your chance to learn about the candidate. Don't be shy. Ask and ask and ask and listen and listen and listen.

When you have finished asking your list of questions, ask the candidate if she has any additional information related to the position that she would like you to know. This gives the applicant the chance to mention or reiterate any strengths she brings to the position. Then ask the candidate if she has any questions for you.

If an applicant voluntarily offers information that you would never ask for legal reasons (see the quiz questions in figure 8.1), human resources specialists recommend that you not write down the information she volunteers. Instead, guide the interview back to issues specifically related to the job.

At the end of the interview, thank the applicant for her interest in the position, outline what will happen next, and give the applicant a sense of when you will make your decision.

After the Interview

After the interview, note your impressions of the job candidate and her answers to the questions you posed. Complete this task as soon as possible after the interview, particularly when you are interviewing more than one applicant.

Once you have completed all the interviews and are assessing the results to decide which candidate best fits the requirements for the position, remember to check applicants' references if you have not already done so. Many organizations require that supervisors check references prior to making an employment offer. Even if this is not a requirement at your library, never offer a position to a candidate without checking his or her references first.

Reference Checks

Conducting reference checks will give you added insight on an applicant's personal characteristics and past job performance (i.e., reliability, attendance, quality of work) and allow you to verify the information that the candidate provided. Make sure you obtain the applicant's consent before calling a former or current employer. If possible, work with your library or larger organization's human resources department to revise application forms so as to require applicants to list all previous employers, dates of employment, positions held, names of supervisors, and reasons for departure. It is important to be consistent in conducting all reference checks.

When checking references, keep notes of the names contacted, what questions were asked, and what answers you received. And, as with interview questions for applicants, the same questions should be asked for each applicant's references. Developing a standardized form or script can make reference checks very systematic and easy to conduct. Use the reference check to verify factual information, such as dates of employment. Figure 8.2 shows a sample script for a reference check.

Background Checks

Some libraries, or the larger organizations to which they report—college or university campuses, city or town governments, and so on—require criminal background checks for all new employees. Some organizations require background checks for certain positions; for example, employees working with children and employees with money-handling responsibilities. Be sure to know the requirements in your organization. Work closely with your human resources office to be sure that the information needed for a background check and any release forms needed for the information are filled out correctly. Never offer a position until the results of a background check are known. Be sure that any negotiations about the position make it clear that a job offer will be dependent upon the results of the criminal background check.

FIGURE 8.2   SAMPLE SCRIPT FOR A REFERENCE CHECK [WEB]

Hello. My name is [your name] and I work at [Such-and-Such Library]. We are interviewing for a [digital reference librarian position] and would like to verify employment information on [applicant's name], who was employed by you from [beginning date] until [ending date].

- What was the nature of his or her job?
- What did you think of his or her work?
- What are his or her strong points?
- What are his or her weak points?
- How did he or she get along with other people?
- Would you comment on his or her attendance; dependability; ability to take on responsibility; ability to follow instructions; degree of supervision needed; overall attitude; quality of work; quantity of work?
- Why did he or she leave the position?
- Would you reemploy him or her? If no, why not?
- Is there anything else you would like to comment on regarding [applicant's name] employment or job performance?

Negotiating the Offer

When all interviews are finished, comments and input have been collected from all who participated in the interviews, references have been checked, and required background checks have been completed, you are ready for the next step of making the job offer to your top candidate. Prior to contacting the successful candidate, be sure you have all the information you need to make the offer: details on salary, vacation, sick leave, and retirement benefits, as well as start date, moving expenses, and who, besides you, to contact with questions about any of these topics.

For salary, you should know the amount of funding available for the position. In some situations, your organization might have a salary range for positions at certain levels. Sometimes you may have a specific salary you can offer, with no room for negotiation. If the position is part of a union, be sure you are aware of union rules for salary levels. If your organization offers some flexibility with salaries, be sure to consider what staff members in the same type of position are earning. Look at the candidate's years of experience, additional education, and any other factors that might influence the salary that you can offer to the candidate.

For vacation, holidays, sick leave, retirement, and other benefits, be sure you have all the information you need for your conversation. Your organization will likely have a human resources or personnel office to which you can refer the candidate if she has additional questions about these benefits.

Be prepared to suggest a start date, and then be ready to negotiate based on the needs of the candidate. If your search results in a local candidate, someone who lives in the area and will not need to move, you may suggest a start date as soon as you can be ready for the person to start. (See chapter 9 for details on what you will need to be ready on Day 1.) Depending on the type of position, you may have conducted a national search. In this case, your candidate may be moving from another city across the country and will need more than two weeks to relocate. Know what the ideal start date would be from your perspective, and then be prepared to take into account the needs of your successful candidate. Many libraries offer moving expenses for some library positions, particularly librarians moving from out of town to a new position. Be sure you know the policy of your library before you make a commitment.

Sometimes a search is very successful and you may have more than one acceptable candidate. Rank them in priority preference, with a plan to contact the top choice first. Sometimes searches are not successful, and you might have a search with no viable candidates. When this happens, you may want to review the job advertisement and position description and ask colleagues at other libraries if they would review it, too. It may need a rewrite to bring in different types of candidates. If the ad and job description seem acceptable, you might also think about whether you want to reconsider candidates in the initial pool who were not selected to interview, or reopen the search.

Summary

Hiring decisions are some of the most important decisions you will make as a manager or supervisor. You will be most successful when you

carefully think through the requirements of the position

clearly state the job requirements in the ad

ask behavioral questions that are job-related

listen carefully to interviewees

hire talent and train for skills

know your own biases and guard against making decisions
    based on those biases

ask legal questions and avoid non-work-related questions

When you hire the right people for the right jobs, you will have the solid foundation you need for a successful unit or department.

NOTES
1. Beth McNeil, "Managing Work Performance and Career Development: Implications for Human Resources in Academic Libraries," in *Human Resource Management in Today's Academic Library: Meeting Challenges and Creating Opportunities,* ed. Janice Simmons-Welburn and Beth McNeil (Westport, CT: Libraries Unlimited, 2004).
2. Thyra Russell, "Interviewing," in *Practical Help for New Supervisors,* ed. Joan Giesecke (Chicago: American Library Association, 1997).
3. University Libraries, University of Nebraska–Lincoln, internal document on core competency–related interview questions.

9

Orientation and Training

Orientation

First Day on the Job

Training

Mentoring

Summary

Never tell people how to do things. Tell them what to do and they will surprise you with their ingenuity.

—General George S. Patton

NOW THAT THE search is over and you have filled the job opening in your unit, you may believe your work is done. Not quite! You must orient the new employee to your library. An effective orientation will include introductions to current staff and an introduction to policies and procedures. It also provides an opportunity for the new person to begin to get to know the culture of the organization. The new employee's orientation, in particular the first day on the job, can influence how she will feel about the library throughout her employment.[1]

The details of an orientation program will vary depending on the type and size of your library, as well as the nature of the position. However, many libraries share common goals for new employee orientation, as summarized by H. Scott Davis in his book *New Employee Orientation,* including

> To make all new library employees feel welcome and comfortable as they begin the new job;
>
> To provide consistent documentation and interpretation of major library policies and philosophies for all new employees and, in the course of doing so, to strive to avoid "information overload";

To acquaint all new library employees with other library staff and other departments and units within the library system;

To provide continuing orientation support to all new employees during the initial months of their employment through mentoring and other activities;

To tailor individual orientation activities/information according to the varying information needs for different positions within the library and, in doing so, to be mindful of individual differences among new employees in terms of personal experience and educational background;

To emphasize the new employee's role and potential for contributing to the overall mission of the unit/department, division, and library; and, finally,

To call attention to the importance of continuing staff development and the library's commitment to staff training, and to emphasize new employees' share of responsibility in self-initiating/communicating staff development needs to their supervisor.[2]

Orientation

The preparation for an orientation of a new employee should start as soon as you have made a hiring decision, if not before. Planning includes both in-house preparation and communication with your new employee. Your library may have a general orientation for all new employees. Check with your supervisor or the library human resources specialist to find out about the standard orientation procedures in your library.

Before the new employee's first day, you will want to review the position description and the job duties or responsibilities for the position and make any necessary changes. These two documents are crucial to the success of the new employee, both so that she will know what is expected and how her work fits into the larger organization. Carefully plan how you will explain the position and its duties to the new employee.

You may want to consider generational differences when planning the orientation of a new employee. The youngest group of library workers today, born in the late 1970s or later, and often referred to as Generation Y or Nexters, are in general used to learning in a highly interactive way. Like their slightly older coworkers from the Generation X group, they may like to role-play, finding it to be good practice for real-life skills. For example, if you are training Gen Y or Gen X staff to work at a public service desk, role-playing situations with difficult patrons might prove to be a very effective training tool. When orienting employees born in the mid-1960s through 1975 or so, or Generation X, a less structured training plan for orientation may be helpful. If you plan to walk through your library's policy and procedure documents, you might consider instead showing them the files (binders, library staff website, etc.) and encouraging them to review them. Keep in mind that the average Generation X staff member is not afraid to ask questions. Consider providing a list of in-house experts so that when the new employee has a question, she can go directly to the right source for the answer.

For new employees from the Baby Boomer (born between 1946 and 1963) and Veteran (born before 1945) generations, discuss your library's overall goals. Boomers will want to know how they will fit into those goals. Baby Boomers like to see themselves as making a difference and as an important part of a larger, worthwhile effort. When you are discussing the upcoming challenges, convey that you will need their help. Individuals in this age group want to solve problems. Veterans also want to contribute. With them, you may want to convey not only the unit and organization goals, but also tell them the history of the department and the library: where the library is coming from and where it is trying to go. Veterans, more than Baby Boomers and much more than Generation X employees, want to know the policies and guidelines of your unit and library. They will desire a very detailed orientation and training program and will want more structured orientation than younger generations.[3]

If your library has in place a set list of orientation meetings for new employees, you will want to supplement it with sessions pertinent to the particular position. Depending on the nature of the position, and your library's policies, the orientation period may last anywhere from a few weeks to several months. Some meetings can take place during the first week, and others in subsequent weeks. Some details should be handled on the first day at work. Prior to the new employee's first day on the job, you will want to schedule as many meetings as possible for the new employee to meet with colleagues in the unit and in the library. Figure 9.1 shows a sample schedule for a new employee in Tony's department.

Orientation Checklists

As a supervisor, you may find it helpful to use an orientation checklist for new employees. Your library may have a general checklist you can tailor to your unit's needs. If not, develop one for your unit. The checklist might include people to meet within the unit, the library, and outside the library; meetings to attend; and projects or programs with which to become familiar as soon as possible. The checklist may include the names

---

FIGURE 9.1   SAMPLE SCHEDULE FOR AN EMPLOYEE'S FIRST DAY

SOPHIE FISHFEATHER
Library Assistant, Cataloging Unit
Townsville Library

Day 1—Thursday, March 1

8:00 a.m.	Meet Tony Supervisor at library's entry. Introduction to unit: review of orientation schedule. Review of personnel policies, department procedures, and other general information.
10:30 a.m.	Tour of library with Fiona Birdcup (acquisitions assistant)
12 noon	Lunch with Tony Supervisor
1:00 p.m.	Unit staff meeting
2:00 p.m.	Library human resources department (for employment paperwork)
2:45 p.m.	Library director
3:00 p.m.	Walter Bauxbiter (mailroom manager)
3:30 p.m.	T. C. Catman (serials check-in)
4:00 p.m.	Review of first day
5:00 p.m.	End of day one!

---

of those responsible for particular aspects of orientation and whether or not the item or function is required or optional. (See figure 9.2.)

Orientation checklists can be used as a supervisory planning tool prior to the employee's first day of work. They can also serve as the written orientation plan that you give to the new employee during your first meeting with her. Some checklists, like the one in figure 9.2, note when the meeting or activity should take place. Others are less detailed and serve more as a reminder list of meetings that need to be scheduled, such as the sample list for a new reference librarian in figure 9.3.

Preparations for Arrival

Prior to the new employee's arrival, prepare her work space. Make certain that the basic equipment and office supplies necessary for the position are in place and ready to use. Basic supplies include desk supplies, such as a stapler and scissors, as well as the increasingly necessary ergonomic supplies related to extended computer workstation use. A checklist of supplies for consideration is included at the end of this chapter.

FIGURE 9.2 ORIENTATION CHECKLIST FOR STAFF IN TECHNICAL SERVICES

TECHNICAL SERVICES DEPARTMENT ORIENTATION CHECKLIST

New Employee: Sophie Fishfeather   **Position:** Library Assistant

Unit: Acquisitions Unit   **Start Date:** Thursday, March 1

Function/Activity	Person Responsible	1st Day	1st Week	Subsequent Weeks
Review of orientation schedule	Supervisor	X		
Review position description, job duties, and responsibilities	Supervisor	X		
Review personnel policies				
Hours and scheduling	Supervisor	X		
Time sheets	Supervisor	X		
Breaks	Supervisor	X		
Types of leave	Supervisor	X		
Staff development programs/training	Supervisor	X		
Use of computers and e-mail				
Other	Supervisor	X		
Tour of library	Department	X		
Introduction to e-mail system and log-on	Systems office	X		
Individual meetings with unit staff				
Fiona Birdcup	Supervisor		X	
Jasper Brody	Supervisor		X	
Walter Bauxbiter	Supervisor		X	
T. C. Catman	Supervisor		X	
Individual meetings with staff in other units				
Cataloging supervisor	Supervisor			Week 2
Serials manager	Supervisor			Week 2
Binding manager	Supervisor			Week 3
Etc.	Supervisor			Week 3+
Orientation to computer network	Systems staff		X	
Employment paperwork	Library admin.	X		
Keys	Library admin.	X		
Parking permit	Library admin.		X	
Online catalog training	Supervisor		X	

FIGURE 9.3   ORIENTATION CHECKLIST FOR A REFERENCE LIBRARIAN   WEB

Schedule meeting with one department head each week:

- ☐ Access services
- ☐ Technical services
- ☐ Systems
- ☐ Digital initiatives

Schedule meeting with one unit head each week:

- ☐ Circulation
- ☐ Interlibrary loan
- ☐ Microforms
- ☐ Documents
- ☐ Binding

Regularly scheduled meetings to add to calendar:

- ☐ Reference dept. meetings (1st and 3rd Thursdays at 1:00 p.m.)
- ☐ Digital initiatives dept. meetings (4th Wednesday at 3:00 p.m.)
- ☐ Library faculty meetings (1st Tuesday in September, December, February, and May at 9:00 a.m.)

Other meetings to schedule after librarian is on board:

- ☐ Academic departments

And last, make arrangements with the new employee regarding what time she should report to work on the first day and where you will meet her. Share her orientation schedule with her. If this is not possible, at least provide a schedule for her first day, with confirmation of where and when she should report.

First Day on the Job

Setting the right tone for the new person's first day on the job is crucial. At the end of the first day, the new person should feel welcomed to the unit and library and valued for the skills she brings to the job. She should know the general plan for her orientation and what training to expect in the next few weeks.

A person beginning a new job may be anxious about many things that first day, including everything from how to remember the names of all the people she will meet to the scope of her job duties. Your goal is to alleviate that anxiety. When you first meet the new employee, greet her warmly and welcome her to the library. Remind the new employee of your name. Let her know how to address you:

> Good morning. I'm Tony Supervisor. It's good to see you again. We're so glad you're joining us here at the library. As I mentioned during your interview, I'm the manager of cataloging and I will be your supervisor. Please call me Tony. May I call you Sophie?

If your name is difficult to pronounce, repeat it and, if possible, provide a key to remembering how to pronounce it. Keep this in mind, as well, as you make introductions to other staff throughout the day.

Review the orientation and training schedule with the new employee. Explain whom she will be meeting with and the purpose of each meeting. Note any regular standing meetings that the new employee should plan to attend.

Introduce the new person to members of the unit and to other staff with whom she will work frequently. On the first day, these introductions can be brief. Your orientation schedule will include time for in-depth meetings, and explaining the staff member's work and her role in the department, later in the orientation period.

The first day on the job should include a tour of the unit or department and the library. You or another member of the unit can lead the tour. Try to show the employee as much of the library as possible without overwhelming her. During the tour, you may encounter additional staff members to introduce to the new employee. Depending on the size of your library, you may decide to tailor the tour, perhaps saving some parts for future days. At the very minimum, you should make sure the employee knows how to find the bathroom, break room, and how to navigate to and from the unit from the library's entry.

Although you may have shared the position description with the new employee at the time of her interview, you should review it with her again in detail on her first day. Discuss each job duty, the tasks and routines associated with it, and how performance on each duty will be evaluated.

At some point during the first day, you will want to provide time for the employee to work with your human resources staff to complete appropriate paperwork in order to ensure timely payment of salary or wages. Some libraries may handle these details prior to the first day on the job. Check with your human resources specialist to learn the procedures in your library.

And finally, keep in mind that your new employee will need time to familiarize herself with her new work space and time to review the documentation that you have shared during the day. This "downtime" will allow the employee an opportunity to reflect on the meetings and activities of her first day on the job.

Training

Training is an integral part of orientation. During your initial discussions with the new employee, including the review of the orientation schedule and the position documents, the new employee should learn more about the specific training necessary for the position. A focus on training during this initial orientation will signify to the employee that you value her ongoing development. Increasingly, the jobs of librarians and library staff members are changing to meet the needs of library users. Most positions in today's libraries require ongoing training to stay up-to-date with new software versions, web resources, and other electronic resources. During orientation, it will be important to share with a new staff member your expectations for attendance at staff development and training events.

As a supervisor, you may be responsible for much of the position-specific training for a new employee. As you are considering the content for the training, you may want to think about how to best deliver the training and what to teach the new employee first. Knowing the employee's preferred learning style will help. Questions to consider include: "Will the content be understood more easily and retained longer if the employee sees a videotape, completes a workbook, or listens to a presentation? In what sequence should new information be presented? What should we teach the new employee first—how to search a book order or how to process a vendor list? Does it matter?"[4]

Many libraries also provide library-wide training for library staff and librarians. Sometimes this training is organized and developed by the library administration or by a staff development committee or team. Training may be on topics such as customer service, facilitation skills, communication skills, basic library skills, leadership development, measurement and assessment, team building, technical skills, or other efforts related to library-wide goals or library administration initiatives. The library administration may encourage, and sometimes require, staff participation at training on issues related to organizational culture. Some libraries have developed training or career development plans tailored to individual staff members. Whether you are developing a single training session to address one topic or a multisession training program for a new employee, effective training programs include the following steps:

analyzing needs	formulating instructional strategies
describing the task	sequencing
analyzing the task	developing materials
writing objectives	preparing evaluations[5]
developing tests	

By becoming familiar with the staff development planning and opportunities in your library, you will be able to plan for appropriate orientation and ongoing training for the staff you supervise.

Mentoring

Mentoring is an important aspect of work in libraries and is sometimes overlooked in the planning process for orientation and training. Sometimes organizations have formal mentoring programs to assist employees throughout their careers. These programs may involve formal pairings of employees, with an experienced employee mentoring a new employee or an employee moving into a new role. Sometimes mentoring relationships develop much less formally, between two people who "click" and agree to be in a mentoring relationship. Sometimes mentoring relationships are short term, with a specific focus or goal to achieve; other times mentoring relationships last for years. As a supervisor, be prepared to serve as mentor to your employees and help them to develop mentoring relationships with others in your library or in the library field.

Summary

A carefully planned orientation program will help your employees begin their jobs on a positive note and with the information they need to succeed. Remember to include the following in your plans.

Before the first day

Communicate with the employee regarding the logistical issues of the first day on the job: when and where to report, work schedule or hours, where to park, and so on

Prepare the work area with supplies

Pencils, pens	*Stapler*
Scissors	*Paper*
Notepads	*Mouse pad*
Wrist rest	*Wastebasket*
Phone books	*Recycle bin*
Staff directory with phone, e-mail, office address information	

Assess equipment needs

Computer workstation	*Printer*
Headphones	*Flash drive or thumb drive, and so on*

First day

Meet and welcome new employee

Introduce employee to coworkers

Provide tour of library

Review job duties and responsibilities

Explain e-mail and phone access

Complete employment paperwork

First week

Discuss and review unit or department policies

Provide follow-up tours, depending on size of library

Discuss library goals and objectives, library-wide policies

Training in core job areas

Subsequent weeks

Meet with pertinent staff members and departments

Ongoing training

NOTES

1. Katherine Branch, "Orienting the New Library Employee," in *Practical Help for New Supervisors,* ed. Joan Giesecke (Chicago: American Library Association, 1997), 15–23.
2. H. Scott Davis, *New Employee Orientation: A How-to-Do-It Manual for Librarians* (New York: Neal-Schuman, 1994), x.
3. Ron Zemke, Claire Raines, and Bob Bilipczak, *Generations at Work: Managing the Clash of Veterans, Boomers, Xers, and Nexters in Your Workplace* (New York: AMACOM, 1999).
4. Pat L. Weaver-Meyers, "Creating Effective Training Programs," in *Staff Development: A Practical Guide,* 3rd ed., ed. Elizabeth Fuseler Avery, Terry Dahlin, and Deborah Carver (Chicago: American Library Association, 2001), 125.
5. Ibid., 125–28.

Planning and Organizing Work

NOW THAT YOU are a supervisor, you are responsible for planning and organizing the work of your unit. Planning can involve everything from day-to-day prioritizing of projects and activities for you and your staff to decision making on long-term projects and activities for your unit to meet your larger organization's goals. Planning is an ongoing process that must evolve as the needs of your organization change. You will need to be flexible and be a model of adaptability and flexibility for the staff you supervise, so that they become accustomed to the rapidly changing environment of today's libraries.

Setting Goals and Objectives

As the leader of your unit, you are responsible for ensuring that your unit has goals to accomplish. Goals need to be more than broad statements that sound like the proverbial "Mom and apple pie" approach to goal setting. Rather, goals need to be practical activities that the unit can and should accomplish. These activities help order the efforts of the unit by providing a direction for the unit to follow. Without goals, the unit will not have direction and its members will not know if they are accomplishing tasks that will help the organization.

The goals of your unit or department should relate to the overall goals of your library or larger organization. Many libraries develop library-wide goals as part of a strategic planning process, an annual planning process, or some other planning effort. These goals may span several years, with new objectives developed for each year. Departmental goals can follow this pattern. As a supervisor working with your unit, you will identify the goals of your unit or department, establish priorities among those goals, and identify the tasks that must be accomplished to meet the goals. It is important to include members of the unit in the goal-setting and objective-identification process. Staff in the unit provide firsthand knowledge and experience that can help shape the objectives for the unit and set measurable objectives.

Developing objectives for the unit becomes the basis for unitwide as well as individual planning. Good objectives have the following characteristics, as summarized in the mnemonic SMART: Specific, Measurable, Achievable, Relevant, and Time-bound.[1]

An objective outlines specifically what is to be done (S) and what measures you will use to determine that an objective has been reached (M). The objective should provide the unit with a challenge that can be met (A). You don't want to write objectives that will serve to frustrate your unit because they cannot be completed. Objectives should support the mission, vision, and goals of the organization (R) and have a time frame attached to them (T). An objective for a reference department could be "to plan and implement a 24/7 online chat reference service within six months." The objective is specific (chat service, 24/7), measurable (either the service is implemented or it isn't), achievable (assuming the resources are available), relevant (it relates to user needs), and has a time frame (implement within six months).

Once you have identified goals and established priorities for your unit, you can determine your own personal goals and work with staff to determine their goals. You will need to decide who will perform each task, how often the task will need to be performed, and the timetables and deadlines for each task. Staff will need to understand the rewards for accomplishing the tasks and goals, as well as the implications for themselves and the department if tasks are not accomplished and goals are not met.

Remember to review and update your unit's action plans regularly, perhaps quarterly, to be sure you are on track for the year. By keeping your focus on overall objectives, you can be sure your unit does not get sidetracked by mundane details and day-to-day tasks and can accomplish the larger projects that bring success for your unit.

Planning does not need to be an arduous process or one that induces sleep on the part of participants. As a supervisor, you can keep the process focused and efficient by following a few key steps.[2] These steps are the core of most planning processes. The first step is to list the external and internal forces that impact the unit. While many planning processes include a rather elaborate procedure for completing an environmental scan, you can do this with your unit rather easily as you think through the information you already know about your environment. Second, review the strategic initiatives of your organization. As a supervisor, you are not starting with a blank page when doing planning. You want to be sure your plans fit within the larger organization. Third, develop a list of activities for the unit that blend with the strategic initiatives of the organization. Finally, review the list of activities with the list of internal and external forces to develop a feasible set of objectives for your unit. You don't want to create objectives that cannot be completed, given the environment in which you operate.

How can this simpler process work for your unit? For Tony, the cataloging unit head, this process will make it possible for him to create goals for his unit in two focused meetings. In the first meeting with his unit, Tony and the group consider the external and internal forces that impact their work. External forces can include the economic outlook for the organization, changes in the OCLC cataloging system (including changes in network structure), changes in MARC standards, and the development and use of different metadata schemes (including Dublin Core). Internal forces can include budget reductions, possible restructuring proposals for the organization, and possible personnel changes as staff approach retirement. The group also reviews the organization's strategic priorities, which could include decreasing expenditures, enhancing access to information resources, and ensuring a user-relevant catalog.

In the second meeting, Tony and the group develop goals for the unit, such as incorporating metadata schemes such as Dublin Core into the catalog for image collections, or reducing the use of paper by using more online files and wikis for communication among the unit's members. These objectives are specific and provide direction for the unit for the year. Finally, Tony and the group review the goals along with the internal and external forces to ensure that the objectives are practical and achievable given the possible environmental changes. By staying focused on key activities, keeping conversations centered on achievable ideas, and not spending time on brainstorming ideas that cannot possibly be implemented, Tony and his unit can create doable plans in a relatively short time.

Organizing the Work of Others

As a unit head or supervisor, you will need to make decisions about how the work of your unit will be accomplished: what needs to be done and who will do it. As you will learn, most likely on your first day as a supervisor, each staff person is unique. Staff members will have varying work styles, and supervisors must understand, recognize, and accommodate the different work styles of the people they supervise. The good news is that while individuals exhibit unique traits, there are some similarities in work style preferences. Some employees will prefer a great deal of structure; others will find too much structure to be stifling. Depending on your own style, you may need to adjust the way that you work with individual staff members. (See chapter 4 on motivation and chapter 6 on diversity for more about different work styles.)

Work style preferences can be generalized into two groups: creative types and structured types. As a supervisor, you will observe very different behaviors from these groups, and you may need to adjust your interactions with staff members of each type, depending on your own work style preference.

If you prefer a more structured environment, you may be frustrated when you supervise creative types even when the work is completed successfully. For example, creative staff members sometimes appear disorganized, yet often accomplish a great deal. The more structural aspects of work life, such as routines or work guidelines, may seem too mundane for creative types to follow. On the other hand, your creative staff members will bring new ideas to stale routines and, if you let them, help you to rethink the work of your unit.

To support creative staff members and help them to be productive, you might do the following:

Present assignments in general terms, explaining the desired end result but allowing employees the latitude to find their own ways to that result. Establish time lines to keep productivity on track but don't structure the work process.

Allow people to express risky ideas without immediately shooting them down. Saying "Let me play devil's advocate" is the surest way to cut creative thinking off at the knees because it sets a negative tone. Instead, ask clarifying questions, or begin with a phrase such as "I am not in disagreement with the idea, but want to explore some questions I have." This type of opening sends a more positive message and opens the door to discussion.

Let people work through their mistakes to find their own solutions and allow time for this as part of the creative process. It takes a lot of coal to make diamonds.

Learn how to praise someone's efforts without focusing on the result or product you want those efforts to generate.

Ask employees what you can do to provide a stimulating and
supportive environment. You might be surprised at how
simple some of their requests will be.

Sponsor workshops conducted by outside resources. Creative
people are always looking to broaden the base of
their knowledge and expertise. New faces bring fresh
perspectives. Employees are sometimes more willing to
question and raise issues with outsiders than they are with
internal trainers or consultants.[3]

If you are a creative manager, supervising a staff person who wants or
even requires structure can be frustrating. On the other hand, structural
types are the people you want to help plan complex projects, as they are
very skilled at breaking projects into logical steps. They are good at imple-
mentation as well, and after understanding what the work is and what
their role is in the process, they will meet deadlines. Often their work
spaces are neat and functional, and if necessary someone else can step
into their job.

To help you determine how best to work with a person who needs
structure, consider the following:

Start by laying out specific tasks and the small goals that
must be accomplished by the end of the day. Be sure the
employee has the necessary tools to complete the tasks
and knows how to use them.

Identify common problems that might arise and establish a
procedure for dealing with them. Some employees find
it useful to have a chart or diagram that outlines the
priorities and procedures, while others might just take
notes.

Meet with the employee at the end of the day to discuss how
he approached the tasks and what actually got finished.
Communication about expectations, and what worked and
didn't work, is critical here.

Establish procedures for identifying and addressing
emergencies and unexpected changes in priorities. At
first, this might mean having the employee come to you
whenever work deviates from the planned schedule. As
the employee becomes more skilled in structuring and
adjusting priorities, the procedures might shift to general
guidelines for when to contact you and when to proceed
without assistance.

Over time and as the employee's comfort with the structure progresses, designate daily tasks as part of the employee's routine, with the employee responsible for making them part of the workweek with less monitoring from the manager.

Be a good model. Show employees how you prioritize your day, and then ask them to tell you how they would in turn prioritize their own. Then compare and show them how to make adjustments as needed.

Follow up to see what works and what doesn't, first on a daily and then on a less frequent (but no less than weekly) basis.[4]

Planning a Day

In addition to planning the overall work of the unit, you also need to keep track of planning your own days and your own tasks. David Allen suggests that each day there are three types of activities you might engage in:

doing predefined work

doing work as it shows up

defining your work

Predefined Work

If you are taking action on items from your "to do" list or your next-action list, you are doing predefined work. That is, you are working on tasks that you previously determined need to be worked on. This might include preparation for a meeting with a staff member, drafting performance evaluations, and making or returning phone calls.

On-the-Spot Work

Some days it will seem as if you are not accomplishing anything from your list of tasks that need to be worked on because you have many interruptions. These interruptions, which Allen describes as doing work as it shows up, involve anything that comes up unexpectedly: a staff member stops by to talk with you about a workflow problem, or your boss needs some budget figures for an emergency meeting the next morning. When you spend time on these interactions or tasks, you have prioritized these tasks, unconsciously or consciously, as more important than anything else you planned to do at that time on that day.

Defining Your Work

Most library employees already spend time each day checking e-mail messages, reading paper mail, reading or writing meeting minutes, and responding to phone messages and voice mail. As a supervisor, you will add supervising staff and planning projects to this list. Some of these activities you will finish; many others will involve identifying action items or tasks that you will need to accomplish sometime. These daily tasks, most of which are routine happenings each and every day for supervisors, are what Allen calls defining your work. As you work your way through them, you will be adding items to your lists of tasks to accomplish.[5]

For example, it's late Friday afternoon and Gina, head of the reference department, is planning her work for the next week. She has three management meetings and a department meeting on her calendar. She also has individual meetings with five of her staff and she has two desk shifts. She examines her schedule to identify blocks of time when she can work on projects.

On her "to do" list she has three projects: prepare the unit equipment request, write two performance evaluations, and begin planning for a shift of the reference collection where it is becoming too crowded to shelve.

Next, she notes deadlines for the projects. The equipment request is due Tuesday, so she schedules a meeting with herself on Monday to ensure some uninterrupted time to work on the request. The evaluations are due in two weeks, so Gina knows she can work on these as time permits. The shift of the reference collection will need to be done soon, so she wants to be sure that she has an outline of the process by the end of next week. The reference collection shift includes coordinating activities with the access services department, so Gina includes time for meetings with her counterpart in access services to develop a joint process for the project.

By identifying a few key projects that need to be done and setting preliminary times to work on the projects, Gina has a good chance of getting the projects done. Without setting aside time for these projects, Gina could find her days taken up with daily tasks and interruptions that keep her from getting her own tasks done.

Meeting Deadlines

Deadlines are a fact of life. Without them, most people would not accomplish very much. In your role of supervisor, you will work with staff to determine the appropriate steps to meet deadlines.

For projects with a fixed deadline, one planning technique is backward planning. With backward planning, you start with the deadline and plan backward to the present time, developing a timetable listing the steps in the process. To do backward planning, you begin with the end event.

1. Make a list of tasks that must be accomplished before the deadline or event.

2. Working backward with a calendar, start with the last step.

3. Write the last step on the calendar and note any tasks that need to be accomplished by specific dates to make the last step possible.

4. Repeat #3 with the next-to-last step. Note related tasks.

5. Repeat #4 with next steps until you reach the first step.

6. Determine deadlines for each step.

7. Delegate related tasks to appropriate staff.

Backward planning, with deadlines for each step and delegation of steps to appropriate people, will help to ensure that no important steps or components of the process are overlooked. Also, backward planning will help all involved to know their role and responsibility and how much time it will take to complete the necessary tasks efficiently and effectively.

Projects where backward planning might be appropriate include an event that must happen on a certain day and where several staff members must participate in the project for it to be successful. For example, you are the cataloging supervisor and you learn that an upgrade to the cataloging module of your online catalog system is scheduled for the end of the year. Once the date of the upgrade has been determined, you can plan backward from that date to make sure that everything is in place in time for the upgrade. Another example where backward planning could be effective is at the library circulation desk. Each semester, your unit prepares for the first day of the new semester, when records for new library users will be added to the online system. This year, everyone on campus will have a new ID card with a new identifying bar code. How much time do you have to make the necessary adjustments to routines? Who do you need to involve in the discussions? What other campus units use the bar code and for what data? Answering these questions will help you as you develop your backward-planning outline.

Backward planning can also be used for smaller initiatives and for planning with staff members who work better when they have a structured workflow to follow.

Planning for Change

Many steps are necessary for successful change. For change to be truly successful, those involved must be able to see and understand why change is necessary. Change must be reinforced along the way. John Kotter and Holger Rathgeber propose an eight-step process for successful change:

Create a sense of urgency

Pull together the guiding team

Develop the change vision and strategy

Communicate for understanding and buy-in

Empower others to act

Produce short-term wins

Don't let up

Create a new culture[6]

Tony walks into his regular biweekly meeting with the library director with his usual agenda items, expecting a typical meeting to review the budget and expenditures. Within seconds, though, he realizes something is amiss. Gina knocks on the director's door and pops her head in to ask if she's got the time wrong. Hasn't the director just called Gina to ask her to come by? Gina and Tony look at each other, wondering what's up. Their director is uncharacteristically rattled! Finally, she explains: she's just had a call from the budget office and learned that the university must immediately cut 20 percent from its operating budget; the library must make the cut in the next two months and plan for an ongoing cut of 10 percent for the next year's budget, which opens in four months.

Time is short! The director has created a sense of urgency—the library must have a plan in place within two months. During the next two hours, the director outlines the situation and she works with Tony and Gina (pulling together the guiding team) to decide how to handle the cuts (vision and strategy). They identify immediate cuts and develop a plan for determining the rest of the cuts, which will involve staff throughout the organization.

The director calls a staff meeting for the following day. All staff attend and she explains the situation: they must reduce costs and plan for a smaller budget for the next year. The director outlines the cuts that she, Tony, and Gina have determined and asks all staff to work with their supervisor (Tony or Gina) to find ways to meet the rest of the necessary cuts. All three—the director, Tony, and Gina—communicate with the staff for understanding and buy-in.

Tony asks his cataloging staff to carefully review processing expenses and suggest short-term and long-term solutions to the funding shortfall. He asks that everyone take forty-eight hours to assess and then reconvene with their ideas. Gina meets immediately with her reference staff and asks them to focus on resources that duplicate other resources. Her group members agree to reconvene in one week with their ideas. Gina and Tony empower their staff to act.

Both Tony's and Gina's groups identify some quick fixes immediately, including drastically reducing binding and discontinuing print subscriptions for titles in large aggregator databases. All recognize these are not easy decisions, but they are decisions that must be made for the library to meet its budgetary obligations and so are successes in this change process. Gina and Tony now must find ways to continue to lead the change effort, helping staff to find additional ways to trim expenses. Once the initial cost-saving measures are determined, Gina and Tony will work with staff to continually review processes and procedures to be sure they create a new culture, one that makes new processes stick and helps everyone to be ready for future changes.

Time Management

Are you managing your time or is your time managing you? You may find that you ask yourself this question, as well as asking it of your staff. Much of what was discussed in the sections on setting objectives and meeting deadlines will help you to manage your time and the time of those who report to you. If reviewed regularly, calendars and action lists serve as effective time management tools for many people. Another technique, daily "to do" listing, is a universal of traditional time management training.

Key points for successful "to do" listing include

Each and every day make a daily list of "to do" items. Make it a habit.

Add items from previous days that need follow-up.

Prioritize tasks.

Batch similar tasks.

Keep "to do" readings on hand for when you have a few free moments.

At the end of the day, use today's "to do" list to write tomorrow's "to do" list.[7]

Some management experts regard traditional "to do" lists as wastes of time. For example, David Allen prefers developing several lists, such as action lists, waiting-for lists, project lists, checklists, and someday/maybe lists.[8] Online calendar systems can also help you organize your time. You can use the "to do" function in the system to keep track of tasks that need to be done. Systems can also keep track of deadlines and alert you to upcoming activities and meetings. For example, systems available on cell phones, BlackBerrys, and iPhones, just to name a few options, make it possible for you to keep your calendar with you so you can more easily manage your calendar and "to do" lists. You should determine for yourself the best system for you.

Project Management

Lee Cockerell, former executive vice president of operations at the Walt Disney World resort, and now a teacher for the Disney Institute, suggests a slightly different way to keep a "to do" list. He suggests people ask themselves the following questions when reviewing their "to do" lists. First, of everything I have to do in my life, which tasks should I work on today? Second, ask what projects do I start today that will pay off in five or ten years? Finally, what did I do yesterday that I may need to go back and do better? These questions help supervisors think about long-term projects, work-life balance, and improving performance while establishing the list of tasks to do each day.[9]

Other useful time management techniques include time analysis studies and group or team analysis. A time analysis study can be as simple as jotting down your activities during your workday. The format could be a chart with an hour-by-hour analysis of the way you spend each day for a certain time period. (See figure 10.1.) Another option is to use your personal calendar to note all activities worked on during times when you do not have meetings scheduled. This second option works best when your calendar system allows plenty of room for notes. Keeping a log of your activity for a set time period, one week or one month, for example, can be very revealing.

Careful analysis of your personal time log will allow you to see where you are spending your time and whether that time was well spent. Questions you might ask include

Were you doing the right job at the right time?

Could the job have been done at another time more effectively?

Could you have delegated the job to someone else?

What did you do that should not have been done at all?

You may notice a pattern to the interruptions in your day. How are you interrupted the most often? Are the interruptions mostly by telephone? Are they from staff, colleagues, or your boss dropping in to see you? How often do you check your e-mail? Even e-mail, with you controlling when and how often you check it, can be an interruption.

FIGURE 10.1   SAMPLE TIME ANALYSIS LOG   WEB

Time	Activity	Comments/Notes
8:00 a.m.		
8:15 a.m.		
8:30 a.m.		
8:45 a.m.		
9:00 a.m.		
9:15 a.m.		
9:30 a.m.		
9:45 a.m.		
10:00 a.m.		
10:15 a.m.		
10:30 a.m.		
10:45 a.m.		
11:00 a.m.		
11:15 a.m.		
11:30 a.m.		
11:45 a.m.		

Consider the frequency of these interruptions. How important were the interruptions? How long did it take you to get back to the task you were working on? You can control, to a great extent, the nature and type of interruptions. For example, set aside time each day to go through your in-box and to respond to e-mail messages. For some people, checking their e-mail once in the morning and once in the afternoon is adequate. Others may need to do so more frequently. Regardless of your situation, when you check your e-mail, look for urgent messages and tasks that you can finish in less than two minutes. Urgent messages, of course, should be dealt with right away. Quick tasks can be finished and e-mails deleted. Other e-mail

FIGURE 10.2   GROUP TIME ANALYSIS

Staff Member	His or Her Action	Others' Reactions	Plan to Reduce Time Wasting
Bob	Visits with others on the way to and from break	Stop working to visit	Encourage Bob to schedule break times with people he wants to visit with
Gina	Extended telephone conversations	Overhear personal information and are uncomfortable	Remind Gina to limit personal calls
Rhonda	Asks numerous staff the same work procedure questions	Give different details, become frustrated with all the questions	Schedule a set time for Rhonda to visit with her supervisor to ask questions

messages, which require reading or action that will take more time, can be deferred to the block of time you set aside each day for e-mail. This simple change will save you significant time and keep your e-mail in-box better organized.

Another important exercise to help you manage your time, and the time of your staff, is a group or team time analysis. The purpose of this exercise is to focus on what the members of your unit or group do that affects the use of each other's time.

This exercise also requires a simple chart. To do the analysis, list all the people in your unit in the left-hand column. Note their actions. Note your actions. And in the right-hand column, note a plan to reduce time wasting. (See figure 10.2.) A group or team analysis can be used to show how team members' actions both save and waste their colleagues' time.

Summary

The key to a less hectic work life is to organize, plan, and control your time. Annual plans begin with goals, objectives, and action plans with deadlines. Review progress regularly, at least quarterly. Monthly plans flow from the unit's action plans. Add regular activities such as budget preparation deadlines to your list of tasks and projects to be sure you meet your responsibilities. Weekly and daily plans help you keep focused on what needs to be done. Tasks are less likely to fall between the cracks when you keep action lists and "to do" lists.

Check off or delete projects and tasks as you complete them. Celebrate the unit's completion of tasks and projects to help thank staff for their hard work and to reinforce the benefits of planning. Work closely with your staff to develop systems that help them be productive, stay focused, and complete tasks and projects in a timely manner.

NOTES

1. William A. Salmon, *The New Supervisor's Survival Manual* (New York: AMACOM, 1999), 78.
2. C. Patrick Kohrman II, "No Free Lunch: A Condensed Strategic Planning Process," *EDUCAUSE Quarterly* 31, no. 4 (2008): 62–65.
3. Gary McClain and Deborah S. Romaine, *The Everything Managing People Book* (Avon, MA: Adams Media, 2002), 93.
4. David Allen, *Getting Things Done: The Art of Stress-Free Productivity* (New York: Penguin, 2001), 97.
5. Ibid., 50.
6. John Kotter and Holger Rathgeber, *Our Iceberg Is Melting: Changing and Succeeding under Any Conditions* (New York: St. Martin's, 2005), 130–31.
7. Mary Nofsinger, "Managing Work Time," in *Practical Help for New Supervisors,* ed. Joan Giesecke (Chicago: American Library Association, 1997), 83.
8. Allen, *Getting Things Done.*
9. Lee Cockerell, *Creating Magic: 10 Common Sense Leadership Strategies from a Life at Disney* (New York: Doubleday, 2008), 161.

Managing Performance

Standards and Expectations

Performance Evaluation Systems

Academic Environment and Tenure Systems

Unions

Performance Problems

Firing an Employee

Summary

> *High expectations are the key to everything.*
>
> —Sam Walton

HAVE YOU EVER enjoyed a performance evaluation conference? Have you received an evaluation that made you feel inspired to continue to do a good job? Or do you approach the annual evaluation session with the same reluctance many of us approach a visit to the dentist? Why do evaluations seem so painful? How can you as a supervisor create a process so that an annual performance appraisal is viewed as a positive event in your unit?

A good performance appraisal system begins with a clear understanding between the employee and the supervisor about the parameters of the job, the performance expectations, and an understanding of what will happen if performance standards are not met.[1] A clear position description with standards and expectations for each task is crucial. Clear expectations will help new employees understand what they need to do to succeed. Clear expectations also lay the foundation for any actions you may take to reward employees or to address performance concerns. Legally, you need to show that you are being consistent in defining, monitoring, and evaluating performance. Clear job descriptions and standards provide you with the road map you need to demonstrate consistency. Standards also protect both new supervisors and experienced managers from applying expectations in an arbitrary and subjective manner. Rewarding one employee and not another when both meet a given standard will lead to

117

problems for the supervisor. At a minimum, you will be seen as inconsistent and can lose the respect of your unit. At the extreme, you may be guilty of discrimination and could face legal action.

Performance appraisal does not need to be a legal quagmire. Instead of approaching the issue of performance appraisal as an awful burden, try to see this aspect of management as an opportunity to work with the staff in your unit to make the unit excel. How can you do this?

Standards and Expectations

One of the first steps in the process of establishing a positive performance appraisal system is to enlist the participation of your staff in setting standards and expectations. First, learn about your organization's standards and processes. Share these standards with the staff in your unit. Then work with each employee to determine how the standards will apply to his or her work. For example, if your organization has a standard in public service that no more than three legitimate customer complaints per year will be considered satisfactory, then discuss how you will assess a complaint. If a patron yells at a staff member at the desk because the staff member is following a policy the person does not like, as a supervisor you may establish that this type of incident does not constitute a legitimate complaint. However, if the staff member yells back and uses foul language, it will be a legitimate complaint against the staff member. Outlining these types of expectations before an incident occurs will give you a foundation for rewarding positive behavior (staff member did not yell) or addressing negative behavior (staff member did yell). If your organization does not have standards in place for a particular task or position, then you have the opportunity to develop or revise the standards with your staff. Including staff in the discussion will help them both understand and accept the standards you develop. The input from staff must be taken seriously. If you are only asking for input because you think you should, but have no intention of using the staff input, staff will quickly become disillusioned and will see you as arbitrary rather than supportive.

Staff and managers may declare that quantitative expectations do not apply to their positions, that too much of what they do is subjective and cannot be measured. This argument often comes from the public service areas such as reference work or in describing supervisory roles. In these cases, more qualitative standards or outcomes may be needed. For example, for a fund-raising or public relations position, the outcome of an encounter with a donor or with the media may be beyond the person's control. Nevertheless, fulfilling expectations such as writing thank-you notes within seven days of a visit or interview will allow you, as a supervisor, to describe the behaviors the person does control and to evaluate those actions.

In larger organizations where a number of people perform similar tasks, developing standards and expectations helps to create organization-wide expectations. With generic standards in place, the organization is more likely to treat staff consistently among units. The more an organization can show that staff are treated consistently for similar work, the less opportunity there is for the organization to be found guilty of discrimination.

Generic standards should describe duties and tasks, expectations, and the impact of these standards. The standards should be understandable, clear, and meaningful. For example, a generic statement of responsibility for supervisors might look like figure 11.1. The responsibilities listed there are required for a well-functioning and productive unit. A generic statement of duties with expectations for a time and attendance clerk could look like figure 11.2. The challenge for you as a new supervisor is to be as specific as possible in writing standards while not becoming so detailed that the person feels like a cog in a wheel. Staff need direction that contributes to the process of planning workflow rather than step-by-step instructions that take away all need for the person to think.

Standards and expectations should be reviewed annually to be sure they are still relevant to the work and the unit. A change in a software program can result in a change in workflow that then impacts expectations. Unless the expectations are reviewed regularly, they can become less applicable as the environment changes.

Performance Evaluation Systems

Once job descriptions and standards and expectations are in place, you have the beginning of a performance evaluation system. Now is not the time to put these documents away, only to drag them out in a year to see how staff are doing. Instead, these need to be documents you work with and refer to throughout the year. First, verify that the staff are clear about job duties and expectations. For new employees, you need to review this information in the orientation process. Then follow up with employees every few months to be sure they understand how the expectations apply to their positions. In some organizations, the human resources manager will schedule a ninety-day review with each new employee to review the expectations and be sure the employee understands the job. Having someone outside the unit do this review can help unearth misunderstandings the supervisor could miss. For all employees, standards and expectations should be reviewed semiannually to ensure that changes in performance are addressed early and to ensure that changes in expectations that may be needed are handled quickly.

FIGURE 11.1   SAMPLE STATEMENT OF RESPONSIBILITY FOR SUPERVISORS

SUPERVISE THE [SUCH-AND-SUCH] UNIT, CONSISTING OF [NUMBER] FTE (FULL-TIME EQUIVALENT) STAFF

Work with the human resources department to develop replacement ads for open positions.

Conduct job searches for vacant positions, including interviewing.

Make recommendations for hiring staff.

Establish performance expectations and develop position descriptions, reviewing and updating them annually or as needed.

Train staff or ensure that training occurs.

Evaluate progress and performance, offer support, and coach or mentor staff to meet library core competencies.

Meet regularly, both formally and informally, with staff.

Document performance issues.

Prepare written and oral evaluations of staff in the unit and conduct annual and probationary evaluations.

Recommend salary adjustments.

In consultation with supervisor and library administration, conduct disciplinary action or recommend termination for staff when necessary.

Follow all library personnel policies. Attend training programs offered by the human resources department and the library to acquire an essential knowledge of personnel policies.

Impact statement

Strong supervisory and management skills are vital for the smooth operation of the unit, for maintaining a welcoming environment for all staff, and for maintaining a positive library image to the public.

PLAN AND MANAGE WORKFLOW OF THE UNIT, CONSISTING OF [NUMBER] FTE STAFF AND [NUMBER] FTE STUDENT ASSISTANTS.

Develop unit goals and expectations in consultation with others as appropriate.

Develop and review policies and procedures. Recommend and execute changes as needed.

Create written documentation of routines and procedures.

Conduct unit meetings.

Schedule specific job duties, vacations, and so on for the unit.

Monitor unit staff time and attendance.

Delegate work.

Collect and analyze statistics.

Prepare the unit's annual report and other special reports as requested.

Serve as a resource person to resolve difficult and complex problems.

Serve as the contact person for other units and departments.

Impact statement

Responses to and decisions about complex situations influence the library's effectiveness in local and national arenas.

Source: Adapted from the University of Nebraska–Lincoln Libraries' NU Values generic statements, 2003.

FIGURE 11.2   SAMPLE STATEMENT OF RESPONSIBILITY FOR A TIME AND ATTENDANCE CLERK

TIME CARDS

Serve as time and attendance clerk for staff. Review time cards on a biweekly basis, checking for accuracy and completeness. Check for staff signature, total the regular work hours and leave hours, enter correct payroll earnings codes, and sign off on time cards. Send all time cards to the library administration before the appropriate deadline.

Serve as time and attendance clerk for student assistants. Compare time cards against work schedule and bring any discrepancy to the attention of the supervisor. Check time cards for accuracy and completeness. Check for student signature, total the work hours, and sign student time cards. Enter student totals on student payroll sheet. Send all time cards and payroll sheets to the library administration before the appropriate deadline.

Maintain current knowledge of payroll and timekeeping procedures.

Impact statement

Accuracy ensures correct salary payments for hours worked and that time and attendance reporting is correct. Inaccurate reporting will violate library policies. Meeting deadlines allows the library administration to record payments and in turn allows the Payroll Office to process salary payments on time.

Source: Adapted from the University of Nebraska–Lincoln Libraries' NU Values generic statements, 2003.

It is very important that the supervisor clearly communicate changes in policies and procedures as these changes occur. Do not wait for a formal performance review to tell a staff member that the organization's policy has changed.

It is not fair to hold an employee accountable for following a change in policy or procedure if that change has not been clearly communicated to the staff. Sending out a written notice of the change may not be sufficient to guarantee that all employees are fully aware of it. Reviewing changes at a department or unit meeting may be more effective because it will allow employees to ask questions about the changes. This way, both the supervisor and the employees can be sure they understand the changes, understand why the changes have occurred, and have reviewed how the changes impact the unit.[2]

Ongoing Discussion

Discussing job performance can be built into a regular routine with each staff member so that you are keeping communication lines open in your unit. A supervisor should have a fairly formal meeting every two to four weeks with each staff member to review how the job is going, to answer any questions that have arisen, and to ensure that, as a supervisor, you know how your staff are doing. These meetings can be informal in tone but should always give the staff member a chance to report progress and discuss issues. It is also a time when, as a supervisor, you can address any questions or concerns you have. With regular meetings, you can avoid unpleasant surprises and can help staff stay on course. This is also a time to recognize good work, praise staff for successes, and agree to new projects or objectives.

Annual Performance Appraisal

Tony sits down to write his first evaluations for his new staff, most of whom were previously his colleagues. Most of the staff are performing well. Tony knows, however, that Tom has never been a stellar performer, and Tony is surprised to discover there is no documentation to show that Tom is chronically late for work and has been missing his performance standards. Tony realizes he must begin a process to alert Tom to these issues and develop a plan for Tom to improve his performance.

Tony is frustrated because he knows this has been going on for years and yet no one before him has been willing to document the issues. There is no record that Tom has any idea there is a problem. Tony must begin from scratch.

Tony takes a deep breath and begins to write. He notes that the cataloging unit has performance standards and that he has compared the performance standards to Tom's annual report. Tony notes that there is a gap between the standards and what Tom has reported. Tony writes that he will work with Tom this year to develop a plan to improve his performance.

Tony does not mention the chronic lateness problem because there is no written standard that he can apply in this evaluation. Tony assigns Tom an evaluation rating of "needs improvement." Tony knows that Tom will be upset and so he carefully prepares for the oral conference. He plans to provide a copy of the standards and acknowledge that Tom has not been given the standards before. He anticipates the questions that Tom might ask. Tony plans to ask Tom if Tom feels he is meeting the performance expectations and then to ask Tom how he thinks he can improve his performance to meet expectations. If Tom does not have ideas, Tony is prepared to begin a discussion of planning for change. While Tony knows this will not be an easy evaluation, he is confident he is beginning a process in sync with his institution's human resources procedures: giving Tom notice he needs to improve, developing with Tom a plan for improving, giving Tom time to improve, and establishing a paper trail in case Tom's performance does not improve.

Most organizations will have a system for annual performance evaluations. The process may include a standardized form and a numerical rating system. Or the system may use open-ended letters, leaving the process up to the supervisor. No matter what system you use, a good supervisor will write a clear analysis of the staff member's performance. Vague statements that read like a horoscope will not be helpful to the staff member, nor will it provide the employee with any advice on what is working well. You should present a balanced view of the staff member's performance, noting strengths and accomplishments. Emphasizing strengths will help a staff member focus on successes and will help provide a more motivating environment. A performance evaluation is also a means to document any concerns about a person's performance. Again, balance is a key. Do not overemphasize recent experiences or ignore past events. The evaluation should reflect the entire year.

To complete a successful performance evaluation, follow these steps:[3]

1. Review the staff member's position description, standards, and expectations. Be sure you know what the employee is supposed to be doing.

2. Review your notes on the person's performance for the year. Identify major successes and areas of outstanding performance. Note, too, any areas that need improvement.

3. Complete the evaluation form or write the evaluation letter. Be sure to focus on the current year's performance. Note improvements

from the last evaluation. Do not raise past issues that have been resolved more than a year ago. Tie performance to expectations so that the staff member knows how the work he has done is reflected in the evaluation.

4. The evaluation should contain no surprises. If you have not addressed a problem this year, you should not blame the staff member for not improving. You may list this as an area for growth, but it should not adversely affect a staff member's overall rating.

5. Once the form is complete, give it to the staff member to review prior to any discussion about performance. Some organizations will specify how many workdays the staff member has to review a written evaluation prior to an oral conference. Carefully follow your organization's procedures.

6. Plan the oral conference. Do not read the written form to the employee. Rather, decide on strengths to highlight, accomplishments to review, and concerns to discuss.

7. At the oral conference, outline strengths. Note areas of improvement. Answer any questions the staff member may have. Listen carefully to his concerns. Be sure to address any uncertainty, disagreements, or confusion.

8. Review any concerns you have about the person's performance. Discuss plans to address these concerns.

9. Discuss goals and objectives for the coming year. Include plans to address concerns but also include ways to build on the staff member's strengths to improve performance and reach excellence.

10. Close the conference by signing forms as needed. Review any follow-up that is planned.

11. Because performance evaluations are confidential personnel papers, be sure to file the forms as outlined in your organization's procedures immediately after the oral conference. Do not carelessly leave evaluation forms lying around your office. You must keep them safe.

Once the conference is completed and the forms are safely processed, do not ignore performance issues for a year. Do follow-up as needed. Meet regularly with your staff, discuss their accomplishments, and review areas for growth.

Academic Environment and Tenure Systems

Some academic libraries also must contend with an academic-rank-and-tenure framework for their librarians, in addition to an annual evaluation process. When these two systems are well integrated, librarians and library faculty members have a sound understanding of all the components of their positions, including librarianship/teaching, research/scholarship, and service/outreach/extension, and they know how they will be evaluated on their progress. Unfortunately, in some academic libraries the promotion and tenure process is separate from the annual evaluation process, resulting in confusion and difficulty for supervisors when they address performance issues. If you are supervising tenure-track librarians, be sure to understand both campus and library policies relating to tenure and promotion.

Unions

Libraries in union environments may have specific processes and policies relating to performance evaluation and merit salary increases. In some libraries all staff are unionized, while in other situations only certain groups of staff belong to unions. Unions can be in public libraries, academic libraries, and other types. As a supervisor, be sure you know the union situation in your library and become familiar with union policies relating to position classification, compensation, and so on. Communicate regularly with your library administration and union representatives about issues of concern.

Performance Problems

When issues of performance do arise, you need to address the issues quickly. For example, explaining to a staff member that he missed a field on a cataloging record or was late to a desk shift is more meaningful closer to the event, so you are both clear about the actions that were taken. Leaving discussions of concerns about behavior for too long will mean the staff member and you will be less clear about the details of the issue in question.

Although you should address issues as they arise, you also need to take a moment to plan your conversation with the staff member. It is never appropriate to yell at a staff member, whether in the presence of others or not, unless the person is doing something that is hazardous or dangerous to himself or others.

To address a performance issue, you should do the following:[4]

1. First, clarify in your own mind the behavior you want to see from the staff member. Review the standards and expectations for the task in question so you can assess the situation as objectively as possible.

2. Gather facts about the staff member's performance. For example, if attendance is an issue, know how many times the person was late and how that number compares to the standards and expectations.

3. Analyze the facts to determine if the problem can be prevented, if the employee has enough information to do the task, or if the task is too large for one person to do. For example, if you have not trained a staff member to select vendors for ordering books, you cannot fault the person if he does not make choices that are appropriate.

4. Set up a meeting with the employee and develop an outline of what you want to accomplish. Be sure you are clear about the behavioral issues you want to address. Have examples and documentation handy so you can be as objective and clear as possible.

5. Hold the meeting with the staff member. Outline your concern using the facts you have gathered. Be clear but not cruel. You can tell someone they were late three days out of five without being insulting.

6. Ask the employee for his perspective. How does the staff member think he is doing? Does the person acknowledge the problem? Does the person understand the task and how to accomplish the work?

7. With the staff member, develop a plan for improvement. Agree to what changes will be needed to resolve the problem. Set a time to follow up on the issue and review progress.

8. Hold a follow-up session. Has the behavior improved? Are expectations being met? If performance has improved, you and the staff member have been successful in addressing performance. Monitor his work as you would for any other staff member to be sure performance remains satisfactory.

What do you do if performance has not improved? How can you address continued performance issues without getting discouraged? First, find out about your organization's procedure for progressive discipline.

Most organizations will have a step-by-step process for you to follow. Usually, the process involves an oral warning about the problem. Oddly enough, you need to document when you have this conversation and be sure the employee knows the conversation is an oral warning. If a person is coming in to work late, telling the person he needs to watch his attendance and not giving specifics will not be sufficient to serve as the beginning of a disciplinary process. You need to be clear about what is expected and what will happen if the performance does not improve.

The next step is a written warning. Here you document the problem and provide a written copy to the staff member. Develop a time frame for addressing the problem and outline the next steps if the performance does not improve.

Meet regularly to review progress. Employees having problems will need guidance and attention from you to be sure they know when they are making progress. You also need to document a lack of change so you have enough information to move to the next steps in the process.

If all else fails, you may have to recommend that a person be terminated. If you reach this point of the process, be sure you work with your organization's human resources office, your supervisor, and any union representatives that are part of the process.

Firing an Employee

When a staff member does not meet expectations, is not doing the job you need done, and you have documented your efforts to correct the problem, you need to recommend that the person be terminated. While it is not pleasant to have to fire someone, it is also not healthy for the unit if you tolerate poor performance. When you do tolerate poor performance, you force others in the unit to do the work of the inadequate staff member. This will build resentment toward you, and you can lose the respect of your entire unit.

Firing an employee, though, takes careful planning.[5] You want to be sure you have followed all of your organization's policies and procedures, reviewed any pertinent labor agreements, and alerted appropriate officials to the situation. Pick a time to meet with the employee. Many superiors will plan the meeting for the end of the day so the employee can leave the workplace at the end of the meeting.

Because terminating a staff member can be an emotional time, you will want to be sure you have arranged a secure, safe location for the meeting. Determine whether security is needed and, if so, have someone available during the meeting. The night before, be sure all computer work the person has been doing is backed up. Arrange to have passwords and access codes changed as the meeting concludes. You need to protect the unit and the organization should the employee try to harm the organization.

The meeting with the employee can include your supervisor or a representative from your organization's human resources department. Be sure to have at least one person with you to help document the meeting and to help keep the meeting under control.

At the meeting:

1. Briefly review the problems. Do not go into great detail because you do not want to prolong the meeting, nor do you want to make the employee feel worse than needed.

2. Briefly review the steps taken to address the problem.

3. Tell the person that he is being terminated, what pay if any he will receive, and how to get his personal items out of the office. Be as specific as you can be about the arrangements and still be brief.

For example, if a staff member named Richard has failed to maintain a schedule, the meeting might go as follows. You say, "Richard, you and I have met eight times over the past two months to discuss your schedule. You are expected to be at work by 8:30 a.m. You have been arriving fifteen to thirty minutes late over 75 percent of the time. Because you have failed to meet expectations and have been unable to correct the problem, we are notifying you that today is your last day of work. You will receive two weeks severance pay. Juan, our human resources person, will accompany you to your desk so you can pack up your things and leave."

Richard may become emotional, may declare the process is unfair, or may do very little. You should be careful not to debate the process with Richard and to stay as calm as possible. Once Richard has regained his composure, have someone escort him to his desk and help him pack. Alternately, you may make arrangements for Richard to pack his belongings after work hours. In any case, follow your organization's routine and procedures for these situations.

Remember, this meeting is not about you. You should avoid telling the staff member how bad you feel or how hard it is for you to fire someone. The staff member is unlikely to care how you feel and could resent you for focusing on your feelings instead of the staff member's situation. Be empathetic and professional as you conduct the meeting.

While terminating an employee is an unpleasant task for a supervisor, if you have followed the organization's procedures, tried to work with the staff member, and been clear about the consequences of not meeting expectations, you will know that you tried your best to resolve the issue.

When performance is a regular topic of discussion, it becomes less burdensome to you and to the staff member. The discussion becomes a way to build on performance and to encourage staff growth. The annual evaluation becomes a time to reflect on past accomplishments and plan future direction. When an evaluation is part of an ongoing process, such discussions may not seem like fun, but they will not be as burdensome as you may have feared they would be.

Summary

Performance appraisal begins with a clear job description and understandable standards and expectations. Performance discussions should be an ongoing part of your regular communication with your staff. Address issues quickly. Give praise and recognition regularly. Annual performance appraisals can be a productive time to discuss goals and objectives. They do not need to be a painful, burdensome process. While terminating an employee can be painful, if you carefully follow your organization's rules and procedures, you can make the process less difficult for everyone involved.

NOTES
1. Gary McClain and Deborah S. Romaine, *The Everything Managing People Book* (Avon, MA: Adams Media, 2002), 177.
2. Joan Giesecke, "Appraising Performance," in *Practical Help for New Supervisors,* ed. Joan Giesecke (Chicago: American Library Association, 1997), 26–27.
3. Ibid., 30–31.
4. Ibid., 27–29.
5. McClain and Romaine, *Everything Managing People Book,* 177.

Budgeting Basics

SHORTLY AFTER BEGINNING work, Gina, head of reference, and Tony, head of cataloging, meet to have coffee. Gina has just received a budget report for her department and is confused about what she is supposed to do with the information she has been given. Because Tony has been promoted from within the libraries, Gina hopes Tony will know more about the budget system than she does. Gina shows the report to Tony and asks him what she should do. Tony looks at the report in confusion. The report Gina received does not look like the reports he has for his unit. They realize that handling their units' budgets is going to take some background work to learn how to interpret the different reports they have and how these reports fit into the library as a whole. Now they have to figure out how to get the information they need. They decide to split up responsibility to gather information and then to meet again to compare notes.

The Big Picture

As a supervisor, you will have responsibility for parts of the overall library budget.[1] You may be responsible for a supply budget, a student wages budget, a salary budget, or a telephone and computer budget. Which aspects of the budget come under your responsibility will vary. However, every supervisor needs to have a basic understanding of the overall institution budget in order to be sure that she is structuring the budget to reflect the larger organization.

It is imperative that unit or departmental budgets fit within the framework of the larger institutional or city/county budget. The overall rules for budgeting will come from the parent organization. These are used by the library administration to develop a budget for the library. Each supervisor then will have responsibility for resources that she controls within her unit. To be effective as a supervisor, you need to understand the overall process used to create budgets before you can effectively design or monitor your unit budget.

Budget Methodologies

There are a variety of budget systems that may be used by the parent institution. Being familiar with these methodologies will be important as you develop your own budget.[2]

Planned program budgeting. A program budget lists all of the costs associated with each program and the results or outputs that the program produces. A program can be a service such as interlibrary loan. Interlibrary loan can be part of a larger unit or an independent unit, but in program budgeting, interlibrary loan services would be a budget category. The budget should include all the expenses associated with the program. For interlibrary loan, this would include such items as salaries, computer costs, OCLC costs, software costs, telephones, fax and scanner costs, supply costs, and even staff development costs. The outputs for interlibrary loan would be the number of items borrowed and the number of items lent to other libraries. In assessing the program, you could determine the cost per output to determine what type of increase you may need to expand the program. In tough budget times, you could use the same data to determine the impact that a decrease in the budget has on the ability of the library to provide the service.

Incremental budgeting. Incremental budgeting is the process of requesting increases to a budget line based on last year's budget and on what is expected to happen in the next year. In a journals budget, for example, the budget request might be based on the amount of money spent on journals plus an average inflation factor. One can also divide the journal budget into different categories that might have different inflation rates and use these different rates to develop a more exact prediction on the cost of journals for the next year. For example, science, technology, and medical (STM) journals from European publishers may have higher price increases than humanities and social sciences journals. Conversely, the STM journals may have limits on inflation rates based on multiyear contracts. In doing the budget, you need to understand these differences and account for this in the budget.

Zero-based budgeting. In zero-based budgeting, each program is evaluated as if it was a new program each year and had no historical budget. That is, the base budget is considered zero and the supervisor develops a new budget each year based on the program costs. Zero-based budgeting encourages an annual evaluation of each program in the library as supervisors consider every cost involved in a particular program.

A library may use more than one budgeting method to put together the overall budget request. The library materials budget may be treated as an incremental budget, with requests for increases based on predicted inflation factors. A new program may be submitted using a program-based budget to identify all of the costs associated with the new program. A zero-based budget may be used when a library needs to decrease costs and is trying to restructure the budget to cope with uncertain financial times. As a supervisor, it is important to work with the overall institution to know what type of budget request you need to put together and what information is needed for decision makers to decide how your unit will be funded.

Expenditures

It is also important to understand the different types of expenditures you may face. Some expenditures, such as utilities, are considered nondiscretionary costs that must be paid and over which most supervisors have little control. While you can effectively work with your unit to decrease utility costs by turning off lights or lowering office thermostats, you are not likely to have responsibility for ensuring that the utility bills are paid.

Some expenditures are more discretionary. These are the budgets that you as a supervisor will be able to influence and control. For example, a budget for student assistants or pages is often the responsibility of a unit supervisor to monitor and to be sure that the unit only spends the amount of money it has been allocated. A reference materials budget is also an example of a discretionary budget that the head of reference can control and, with the reference unit, can determine the titles that will be purchased for the area. Again, the supervisor needs to be sure that expenditures do not exceed the budget allocation.

Often a supervisor is asked to put together a budget request for the next budget cycle. In putting the request together, the supervisor should review the overall goals and objectives for the library as well as the goals for her own unit to be sure that the budget request reflects the priorities of the library as a whole. For example, if the library has made a commitment to expanded electronic reference resources, the head of reference will want to put together a budget that emphasizes electronic resources rather than print resources. For a circulation unit, the request for student assistants to help at the desk should reflect the hours of operation and the duties assigned to the unit. If student assistants sort and shelve materials as well as staffing a desk, the budget request will reflect how much time is needed for these two major duties so that the correct number of students can be hired to cover the unit responsibilities.

The budget request should provide a justification for the items in the budget as well as the dollars requested. Simply listing the dollar figure for student help will not provide the budget decision makers with adequate information to assess the request. The decision makers will want to know what tasks the students will cover, how many hours a week these tasks take, and how the budget will be expended through the year. Will more money be needed as school starts and will less be needed around holidays? This type of question should be answered in the request so the decision makers do not have to guess at why you are requesting the budget you presented.

Also, be sure that your budget request reflects the reality of your unit. Ask yourself what changes have occurred in your unit that impact your budget. Have you stopped using fax machines in favor of e-mail transmission of reports? If so, are you still paying for a telephone line for the fax machine even though it is rarely used? Assessing each item in your request to be sure that it is still needed is an important though often overlooked part of preparing a budget. A sample budget request is shown in figure 12.1.

Budget Reports

While supervisors may not be responsible for using the institutional budget system, they still need to know the basic capabilities of the accounting and reporting system in order to know what questions can be answered from the system reports. For example, if you want to create a history of spending in your unit's equipment budget to show how you have been effective in addressing equipment needs, you will need historical data. Can the central system provide a report for your unit that breaks out your equipment requests? If not, do you have the data within your unit to put the report together? You need to know before you begin planning your budgets what information is available centrally and what information you will need to keep within your unit. On the other hand, you don't want to spend time creating shadow systems or unit-specific systems for reports or data that are available from the central system. It is not in your best interest to spend time and resources re-creating data that are easily available.

FIGURE 12.1 BUDGET REQUEST AND JUSTIFICATION

GIS BUDGET REQUEST 2008–2009   JANUARY 2009

Item	Description	Estimated Price	Running Total	Cost Object
Laptop computer	A laptop will allow me to be more mobile and expand the training and user-support aspect of the program. I will be able to teach GIS metadata and demonstrate the various uses of GIS and the importance of data retention at various departments around campus as well as remote sites.			
Laptop computer	Dell Mobile Precision M6400	2,809.00		2216021051
Total Laptop		**2,809.00**	**2,809.00**	
Software for laptop				
ESRI ArcView	Software	30.00		
ESRI extra media	Premade maps, etc., to use with ArcView	6.00		
ESRI data	Census data preconfigured to work with ESRI ArcView	30.00		
Adobe Design Premium		320.00		
Virus software (AVG Pro)[a]	Replaces Sophos, which causes problems when downloading large data from government sites	60.00		
Snagit	Software to capture images	50.00		
Microsoft Office		130.00		
Wireless fee from Witt[b]	6.42 per month for 12 months	(77.04)	77.04	2716020032001
Total Software		**548.96**	**3,357.96**	**2216021051**

134

Accessories for laptop				
Backpack	Kensington Contour Backpack, Office Depot item #112-056	104.95		
Folding luggage cart	Bay Travel Gear folding luggage cart, Office Depot item #472118	30.00		
Mouse	Dell Travel Mouse	30.00		
Total Accessories		**164.95**	**3,522.91**	**2216021051**
Software upgrades for Public GIS workstations	This order will upgrade the classroom, public workstations, and my desk computer to the latest version of the ESRI GIS software. This version was published in August 2008 and is already available in other GIS labs on campus.			
ESRI ArcView	For public workstations and classrooms [25 @ 30.00 each]	750.00		
Annual renew of ArcInfo license		350.00		
ESRI extra media	Premade maps, etc., to use with ArcView [5 @ 30.00]	150.00		
ESRI data	Census data preconfigured to work with ESRI ArcView [5 @ 6.00]	30.00		
Google Earth Pro[c]	Software	400.00		
Virus software (AVG Pro)	Replaces Sophos, which causes problems when downloading large data from government sites [4 @ 60.00]	240.00		
Total Software Upgrades		**1,920.00**	**5,442.91**	**2216021051**

(cont.)

FIGURE 12.1 BUDGET REQUEST AND JUSTIFICATION (cont.)

Teaching materials	These workbooks will be used to teach beginning workshops on how to use ESRI software in the ESCAPE room. The libraries' GIS training options have filled a much-needed niche for the GIS research community. Designed to supplement UNL's traditional GIS coursework, the workshops are often taken as a "refresher" course as students and faculty begin work on their research projects. In addition, they draw in people who have heard about GIS and are thinking of using it for a project but want to know more before committing to a semester-long course or expensive training from ESRI. (The libraries' workshops are free to students, faculty, and staff.)			
ESRI GIS Tutorial 9.3	Reusable workbooks for classroom and public workstations [24 @ 80.00]	1,920.00		
Content standard	For Digital Geospatial Metadata Workbook [20 @ 10.00]	200.00		
Color photocopying for workshops		100.00		
Total Teaching Materials		**2,220.00**	**7,662.91**	**2216021051**
Content standard	I distribute this workbook and some color handouts as part of my metadata workshops.			
Content standard	For Digital Geospatial Metadata Workbook	300.00		
Total Content Standard		**300.00**	**7,962.91**	**2216021051**
Travel for Mildred Peterson[b]	I have been invited to teach a metadata workshop at the Nebraska GIS/LIS Association biannual conference, April 21–23, Kearney, NE. This is the professional GIS association for Nebraska. Attendees will include several of my colleagues from UNL, CALMIT, and UNL students.			

Nebraska GIS/LIS biannual symposium	Teaching metadata workshop registration fee	(200.00)		2716020024001
Food and lodging	Holiday Inn, Kearney, $100/day	(200.00)		
Total Travel for Mildred Peterson[b]		(400.00)	400.00	2716020024001
GRAND TOTAL	Witt		77.04	2716020032001
GRAND TOTAL	Mildred Peterson		400.00	2716020024001
GRAND TOTAL	Credit Hour Fee GIS		7,562.91	2216021051

[a]ESRI ArcInfo and AVG Pro are annual licenses.

[b]Different fund.

[c]Google Earth Pro has an annual license; however, I believe I can get a grant to have it placed on our public terminals, thus we need only to pay for it one year so I can become familiar with it.

Monitoring Your Budget

Each library will have its own system for reporting on budgets. As a supervisor, you may receive a monthly report that tells you how much money you have spent in a particular category and how much money you have left. Some reports may help track encumbrances (items on order) as well as expenditures so you can be sure you do not overspend your budget because you forgot about ongoing or outstanding commitments. You will want to be sure you understand how to read and interpret these standard budget reports. A sample budget report is shown in figure 12.2.

If the library does not provide you with detailed reports to monitor your budgets, you will want to develop internal systems that help track your funds. A spreadsheet program can be used to develop relatively simple budgets as well as more complex budgets. You can create a relatively simple report for telephone expenses for your unit. In the spreadsheet, you can record monthly use from the telephone bill or central report and subtract the amount from the allocation. The spreadsheet can show the percentage spent. You can review the report for any unusual increases in monthly expenditures that are higher than anticipated. More complex reports can be developed to monitor multiple budget categories using linked spreadsheets. If you are not familiar with spreadsheet software such as Microsoft Excel, you may want to take a course to learn about the system or meet with someone in your library who knows the software. You may want to delegate responsibility for maintaining the budget spreadsheets to someone in your unit who is familiar with this type of software. But remember that as the supervisor you are responsible for the budget, so be sure you understand and review the reports created by others. You are responsible for catching any problems and for ensuring that the reports are accurate and up-to-date.

Returning to Gina and Tony

After a few weeks, Gina and Tony meet again for coffee to go over the budget reports. Gina has learned that her unit is responsible for a reference materials budget, a computer budget, and a student budget. She will be responsible for putting together a request each year for reference resources. She was advised that asking for an inflationary increase would not be an adequate request. Instead, she will need to put together a justification for the types of materials the unit needs, the subject areas to be developed, and the balance of print and electronic resources. Gina has decided that she will have a small committee in the unit help put the budget together, although this had always been done by the supervisor with

FIGURE 12.2   BUDGET REPORT FOR STUDENT ASSISTANTS' WAGES

UNIVERSITY LIBRARIES
BIWEEKLY BUDGET BALANCE SHEET

Department	Budget	Payroll Forward	Payroll	Payroll to Date	Balance	% Used
			1/30–2/12/09	36 Weeks =	69.2%	
Architecture	$24,540.00	$16,700.93	$1,326.86	$18,027.79	$6,512.21	73.5
Archives	$13,330.00	$8,213.14	$667.47	$8,880.61	$4,449.39	66.6
C. Y. Thompson	$61,110.00	$35,924.64	$2,474.40	$38,399.04	$22,710.96	62.8
Circulation	$128,966.00	$78,795.23	$4,879.26	$83,674.49	$45,291.51	64.9
CORS Tech	$16,480.00	$5,839.40	$538.99	$6,378.39	$10,101.61	38.7
Documents	$2,635.00	$1,343.13	$48.78	$1,391.91	$1,243.09	52.8
Engineering	$35,123.00	$19,714.44	$1,534.67	$21,249.11	$13,873.89	60.5
E-text	$6,635.00	$3,119.22	$245.28	$3,364.50	$3,270.50	50.7
Geology	$14,360.00	$8,809.05	$545.43	$9,354.48	$5,005.52	65.1
Math	$6,798.00	$3,970.50	$357.10	$4,327.60	$2,470.40	63.7
Media	$17,510.00	$6,130.50	$460.61	$6,591.11	$10,918.89	37.6
Music	$12,368.00	$6,643.34	$306.51	$6,949.85	$5,418.15	56.2
Preservation	$8,210.00	$6,754.53	$397.13	$7,151.66	$1,058.34	87.1
Res. and Instruct.	$13,744.00	$5,571.26	$522.14	$6,093.40	$7,650.60	44.3
Tech. Services	$13,990.00	$6,550.09	$470.45	$7,020.54	$6,969.46	50.2
All Depts.	$375,799.00	$214,079.40	$14,775.08	$228,854.48	$146,944.52	60.9

the director. Gina wants to be sure that everyone in her unit understands how this important budget works.

Tony has learned that each supervisor will need to track his or her own student budgets. They will receive reports for the library that cover supplies. Equipment budgets will be submitted once a year. The request will include how the equipment will help the unit meet its goals and objectives. He has also learned that all computers are on a four-year rotation cycle, so individual supervisors do not need to budget for desktop computers for staff or for the public areas.

Further, Gina has learned that no one in her unit really understands budgets and spreadsheets. Tony, on the other hand, has a number of staff who are experts in this area. They have agreed to share their expertise, and one of Tony's staff will help one of Gina's staff set up a basic budget system for the unit. They also agreed to have a joint meeting with the library's accountant to review the budget systems they developed in their units, in order to be sure they are creating and maintaining reports that will be compatible with the overall library budget and accounting system.

Summary

Monitoring the budget for your unit is a key task for today's manager. In these uncertain economic times, it is crucial for the supervisor to have accurate records and to anticipate change. If the institution might experience budget reductions, you will be better able to provide advice and help to senior management if you have a good grasp of your unit's budget and performance.

Work closely with your library's budget office to be sure you understand your budget and your budget reports. The budget is an area where it is much better to ask permission and to follow policies and procedures than to go off on your own and risk making budget decisions or purchases that are not permitted.

NOTES
1. For more information on budgeting, see Bob Pymm and Damon Hickey, *Learn Library Management,* 2nd ed. (Friendswood, TX: Total Recall, 2007), 113–20; and Pixey Ann Mosley, *Transitioning from Librarian to Middle Manager* (Westport, CT: Libraries Unlimited, 2004), 67–81.
2. Pymm and Hickey, *Learn Library Management,* 116.

Facilities, Space, and Safety

People You Need to Know

Disaster and Emergency Plans

Summary

CREATING AN INVITING space for users is an important part of ensuring that libraries remain relevant to their user communities. Gone are the days when libraries were sterile, quiet spaces for individual contemplation. Today, successful libraries are busy, active places with a variety of spaces available for users. Patrons can find quiet study areas, computer areas, noisy areas for interactive programs for patrons, and collections space. Space for technical services, special collections areas, and media services may also be part of the building mix. As a supervisor, you may be asked to help evaluate what areas are needed, how space should be allocated, and how space can best be used to enhance the user experience. Where do you begin in order to answer some of these questions?[1]

Supervisors can begin by examining their own unit's area and trying to see the space from the viewpoint of a patron or an employee. Is the area cluttered? Are the shelves in a public area in disarray or overflowing? Can wheelchairs move through the area? Are file cabinets overly full? Are employees' cubicles messy and crowded with library materials and book trucks? If so, you have an easy place to begin. Get rid of the clutter. If you are in a public area, be sure shelves are neat. You may need to weed older materials to make space for new materials. You may need to clean out file cabinets of ephemera. You may need to think creatively about how to re-arrange furniture to make the area accessible to patrons with disabilities.

You may need to encourage staff to organize and clean their own work areas. Have a cleanup day and make a party of the process of cleaning up work spaces. Get everyone in the unit involved so that no one feels singled out for a messy area. You will find that areas that look organized will be easier for patrons to use and provide better spaces for employees to work in.

Once the clutter is gone, it will be easier to evaluate the available space and decide if rearranging it will make the space more effective. Do you have a good arrangement for patron furniture? Can patrons easily find electrical outlets for plugging in laptops and other computer devices? In staff areas, are there good paths to get from one area to another? Are electrical cords strung across walking areas? Are too many pieces of equipment plugged into the same outlet? Are extension cords strung together? All of these issues suggest it is time to seriously consider how the area is arranged in order to create a safe and organized working area.

Many libraries will have someone in charge of facilities and space planning. As a supervisor, you should get to know this person so you can be sure your input is included in planning for your unit's space. The facilities manager can provide you with ideas on how an area can be made more effective and can provide you with advice on the organization's rules and regulations that must be followed. If your organization is implementing procedures to become more environmentally sustainable ("becoming green"), the facilities manager can help you assess how your unit can make changes to support a more environmentally friendly facility. Partnering with a facilities manager in the planning phase for your area can help you avoid having to redo planning later on.

It is also important to include staff in the space-planning process. Librarians and staff can become quite concerned about how their areas may change and how space changes might impact their work. Giving staff an opportunity to participate in the process can help limit their anxiety about change. You may want to begin the planning process by first discussing what functions need to occur in the space and what different types of areas are needed. Do you need to provide a browsing area for patrons to review new books? Do you want to create an area where students can work in groups? In staff areas, do you need a central area for printers and copiers? Do you need a central file area? Listing the functions that are part of the unit and the types of spaces needed will help keep the space discussions focused on the key points to include in planning. Once the list of functions is completed, consider having a floor plan available for staff to experiment with and create different space options. Floor plans can be done on paper with cutouts for furniture, desks, shelving, and other items that are part of the space. Some libraries may want to use a computer program that aids with space planning. No matter how the plans are created, it helps to allow staff some time to try different arrangements until a plan evolves that meets as many of the needs of the unit as possible. Even without significant new resources, a unit can rearrange furnishings in ways that make the area more effective and look refreshed.

Once a plan is in place, you will want to review the signage for the area. What areas need to be easily identified for patrons? How will staff areas be designated? Is there a standard for how rooms are numbered? Including signage in your planning can help ensure you create a design that can then be explained to others and followed easily with appropriate signage.

People You Need to Know

As a supervisor, you will want to know who to call if you have a facilities problem. Get to know the custodial staff for your unit. They can provide you with feedback on how the areas are used. They can also be helpful in suggesting ways that the library staff can work together to keep areas neat and clean. Custodial and maintenance staff can show you where the electrical, utility, or telephone and data closets are and where the water turnoff valves are located. While you may feel you don't need to know this much detail about your area, you never know when you will be the person available to answer questions when repair people are called or disasters occur.

You will need to know how to report facility problems ranging from burned-out lightbulbs to water leaks. Who do you call if there is a telephone service problem or a computer problem? Know who to call if something goes wrong late at night or very early in the morning as well as during the regular business day. Keep these emergency numbers handy so that you can find them easily if an emergency occurs.

There are also a variety of offices that you may need to know, particularly if you are in charge of a building. To be sure that your building or branch conforms to fire and safety codes, it can be helpful to have the local fire marshal tour the area and provide you with advice about how to ensure that your area meets these codes. You may also have access to an environmental health and safety office. This group can help you with information on how to handle a variety of situations, from the storage of hazardous products to how staff should handle air- and blood-borne pathogens.

You may also need to know who handles the maintenance of the exterior of your building, from landscape issues to snow removal. Who picks up the garbage? Does someone provide recycling services? Who do you contact if postal deliveries need to be suspended or changed?

For security reasons, it is important that you know who has keys and access to your area. Does every staff person have a key? Are there offices outside of the library that have keys and access to your building? How can you request keys for new staff members? Who is responsible for locking the area each evening and opening it each day? Knowing these types of details can help you to be sure that you've included all stakeholders in planned changes and you've considered all the various offices and units that need to be involved in any changes you want to make in your facility.

Disaster and Emergency Plans

You will also want to know if your library has a disaster plan and an emergency management plan. Disaster plans will cover what to do if natural disasters such as flooding occur, as well as how to handle emergencies such as a fire in the building.[2]

Furthermore, in today's uncertain world your library or larger organization may have an emergency management plan that covers what to do if someone has a gun, or how to respond to a pandemic outbreak. If your library or organization does not have such plans, work with your administration to create them. At a minimum, be sure you have phone numbers for everyone in your unit if you need to reach them in a hurry and have an agreed-upon place to meet outside if you need to evacuate the building. You will want to be sure you can account for your staff if an emergency occurs.

There are many resources available today to help with disaster planning and emergency management planning. Some libraries will have their disaster plans and emergency plans available on their websites. These sites, along with recent books on handling disasters and disaster preparation, provide a good place to begin your research in this area. While it may not be your primary responsibility to manage or coordinate activities during a disaster, you will want to be familiar with the plans and know how you can provide assistance as needed to keep the library and your staff safe.

Summary

As a supervisor, you may have major responsibility for your library building or you may have little or no direct responsibility for the building. No matter who has responsibility for the overall facility, you are responsible for working with others to be sure your unit and your staff have a safe, secure, and pleasant working environment. Building relationships with the people and offices that are responsible for facility management will make it easier for you to develop a positive working environment that blends well with the overall library and institutional environment. You can enhance the morale of your unit and improve the patron experience by helping to keep your area neat, clean, and inviting for everyone who works in or visits your unit.

NOTES
1. There are a number of handbooks for library facility managers that are also helpful to supervisors throughout the library. See Cheryl Bryan, *Managing Facilities for Results: Optimizing Space for Services* (Chicago: American Library Association, 2007); Carmine J. Trotta and Marcia Trotta, *The Librarian's Facility Management Handbook* (New York: Neal-Schuman, 2001); and Pamela J. Cravey, *Protecting Library Staff, Users, Collections, and Facilities: A How-to-Do-It Manual* (New York: Neal-Schuman, 2001).
2. For a detailed handbook on disaster planning, see Camila A. Alire, *Library Disaster Planning and Recovery Handbook* (New York: Neal-Schuman, 2000).

Managing Meetings

AS A SUPERVISOR, you will attend many meetings. In fact, there may be days when you question whether you ever do anything but attend meetings. It has been estimated that many supervisors spend at least one-third to one-half of their work time in meetings.[1] Often, you will chair or lead meetings. While chairing meetings may sometimes seem like a daunting task, the skills for effective meeting management can be learned.

You will participate in many different types of meetings. Some of your meetings will be regularly scheduled sessions with individual staff members. You may also lead department or unit meetings. Some meetings will be called to address specific topics. Others may be open-ended sessions, with the intent to brainstorm ideas about future directions. You may also find that you are having more virtual meetings, where you and other participants are not in the same location but are connecting via telephone or through the Web. The skills necessary for effective meeting management can apply to many if not all types of meetings, and once you have learned them you will be ready to lead productive meetings.

The Basics of Meetings

There are some key points that apply to any meeting.

Meetings should have a purpose. First, be sure you have a reason to meet. Don't waste people's time by holding a meeting that has no purpose.

Begin meetings on time. We all have busy lives. Starting and ending meetings on time will signal that you value the time of the people at the meetings.

Few meetings should last longer than one hour. Try to keep most meetings to one or two hours. Meetings that go on longer may become repetitive instead of constructive.

Develop and share agendas prior to meetings. Agendas alert participants to the topics to be covered and give participants time to prepare for meaningful discussion.

Meetings with Individual Staff

For supervisors new to an organization, or new to a supervisory role, initial orientation meetings with all unit members are particularly important because they help to set the tone for your work with the unit. A set list of questions to be asked of each member of the unit serves as your agenda for the meetings. While it is not necessary to rigidly follow the list of questions, you should try to cover as many of them as possible. First of all, you need the information the answers will give you, and secondly, staff members will likely compare notes about the meetings. At the initial orientation meeting, it is important to keep the discussion to work-related topics. By asking everyone the same questions, you will be seen as a fair and impartial supervisor, interested in the opinions and viewpoints of all.

Because Gina is both new to her supervisory position and to the organization, the questions she might ask during the orientation meetings may vary slightly from those asked by Tony, who worked in the cataloging unit prior to being promoted to his new position as supervisor. Questions Gina may want to ask include

What are the person's areas of responsibility?

What are the person's top priorities?

Does the person have problems or concerns that Gina should know about?

What are the person's expectations?

How satisfied is the person with the way the department is currently running?

What is the workload? Is it reasonable?

Are there areas of interest that the person would like to pursue?

How satisfied is the person with her current position?

Is the position description up-to-date?

If the person supervises others, does he have concerns about any employees?

Do people have the right equipment and skills to do their jobs?

What resources is the person responsible for?

What other departments does the person work for?

Does the person have concerns about other departments or units that Gina as a manager should be aware of?

What is the person's view of the organization's goals and objectives?

What is the person's career plan?

What changes would the person recommend be considered?

What else does Gina as manager need to know about the person, the department, or the organization?[2]

Because Tony has worked in the cataloging unit prior to becoming a supervisor, he may already know the answers to some of these questions. For example, he likely knows each staff member's responsibilities, the resources available to them, whether they also work in other units or departments, and so on. Tony should take care, however, not to assume that he already knows everything about each of the staff who now report to him.

Depending on your own situation, and how you came to be a supervisor in your current organization, asking these questions of your staff members will help you as you develop an understanding of your unit.

After the initial orientation meetings with staff, you will want to plan for regular meetings with staff members who report directly to you. These meetings will help you to stay up-to-date with the work of your unit, allow you to develop good working relationships with staff, and provide early indications of both successes and failures. As you learn more about your staff members, you will be in a better position to assess their skills, knowledge, and competencies at performance evaluation time, as well as their unique talents that may be instrumental in moving the work of your unit forward.

Individual staff meetings should take place as frequently as necessary to provide you with enough information to know whether a staff member is accomplishing his or her work. Depending on your proximity to staff workstations, you may be able to informally assess staff progress and may find it necessary to meet formally less frequently. In some situations, though, it may be necessary to meet weekly or biweekly. And furthermore, as addressed in the chapter on performance appraisal, addressing and handling performance problems will take additional meetings.

Unit or Department Meetings

Once you have oriented yourself to the unit and learned more about its culture and traditions, it will be much easier to lead unit meetings. While scheduling regular meetings for your unit is important, the necessary frequency of these meetings will vary for several reasons, including the size of your unit, your unit's place in the larger organizational structure, and simply the mechanics of arranging a meeting.

If the unit is small, with fewer than five individuals, frequent formal meetings may be unnecessary, particularly if your work areas are situated near each other and the unit has a culture of close communication and collaboration. Unit members may be in close contact with you and with each other and will need communication solely about events and issues of the larger organization.

However, whether large or small in staff size, any unit that is part of a large organization will need regular communication about the larger organization, and meetings are an effective way to share this information. E-mail has made it much easier to share news, particularly for large organizations. However, as a supervisor you are responsible for communicating news to staff, and regularly scheduled meetings help you increase communication. Unit meetings provide an opportunity for two-way communication: overall organization to unit and vice versa.

For some units, the nature of the work completed by the unit may help determine the frequency of the meetings. In an environment of quickly changing priorities, frequent meetings are crucial. For a unit embarking on a new project or program, regularly scheduled meetings are necessary for planning purposes and to stay on target. Finding a regular meeting time can be a challenge for all supervisors whether they supervise public service operations or behind-the-scenes technical services or systems staff. Supervisors of public service operations, where desks are open and staffed all hours that the library is open, may find it very difficult to schedule a meeting time that works for all staff members. In these situations, a supervisor may need to rely on student workers or assistants to staff desks. Another alternative is for a supervisor to lead the same meeting twice. While this does allow for 100 percent participation, it may lead to miscommunication. Other staff, in units such as technical services or automated systems departments, may have flexible schedules and alternate work sites. Although it may be difficult to plan a unit meeting at least once a month, your job of supervisor will be easier if you can accomplish this.

Preparation for Meetings

Effective preparation is the key for all meetings. As a supervisor, you will often be in a position to determine or define the purpose of the meeting.

Meetings for Information Dissemination

For some meetings, the purpose may be simply to communicate news and directives from the larger organization. These meetings are sometimes called information and briefing meetings.[3] For example, you may schedule meetings with your unit to relay information from a larger departmental or organizational meeting you have attended. The purpose of the meeting is to communicate organizational issues with your unit. Distributing an agenda prior to the meeting, with basic details about the content of the meeting, will convey your purpose to the participants.

Planning, Problem Solving, and Other Issue-Driven Meetings

You may schedule meetings for other purposes than just for communication with unit members. These meetings can be for planning an upcoming project or initiative, problem-solving sessions for new workflow routines, or even decision-making meetings where reaching consensus through group discussion is a necessary function.

For special topic-driven meetings, you will be most successful if you state objectives and expectations for the meeting ahead of time. As with the regular information briefing or communication meetings mentioned above, topic-driven meetings should include an agenda, which should be distributed to all participants prior to the meeting. The agenda can be quite simple or very detailed, depending on the topic and type of the meeting, although it will most often be more detailed than the agenda for a regularly scheduled unit meeting. Figure 14.1 shows a sample agenda for a meeting.

Other important steps to plan for include choosing an appropriate time and location for the meeting and arranging the meeting room in an

---

FIGURE 14.1   SAMPLE MEETING AGENDA

The Technical Services Committee will meet on Tuesday, March 16, at 9:00 a.m. in the library conference room.

AGENDA
1. Approval of minutes from the 3/1 TS Committee meeting.
2. Strategic planning—update from library-wide Planning Committee
3. Review of revised flextime policy
4. Holiday hours
5. Student assistant budgets—reminder of year-end spending
6. Quarterly projects
7. Other
8. Announcements

---

appropriate manner to allow all to participate. For many smaller group meetings, a circle or square will be most conducive to active participation. For larger meetings, it may be necessary to use a different seating arrangement.

The last step in meeting preparation is to be certain that all meeting participants, the staff you supervise, know where and when the meeting will take place. Having regularly scheduled meetings in regular locations takes away the guesswork for staff, and they and you can plan their work and manage their time accordingly.

Conducting the Meeting

At the beginning of the meeting, greet staff and help them to feel welcome. Make sure staff members with special needs have appropriate accommodations. For example, a hearing-impaired staff person may need to sit directly in front of you if he reads lips, and a staff person with mobility concerns may need greater aisle width. These issues should be considered prior to the meeting, when you are determining the meeting room and furniture layout.

Start on time. Through careful attention to the agenda, you will be able to accomplish much during your meeting. Encourage discussion and feedback and keep the conversation on topic. Keep notes during the meeting so that you will be able to write minutes and distribute them to participants and possibly to your supervisor as well. At the conclusion of the meeting, summarize key points, repeat action items and individuals' responsibilities, and set the date, time, and place for the next meeting. And finally, end on time.

Skills for Handling Problem Behaviors during Meetings

Sometimes meetings just don't go well despite your best intentions and attention to all of the pre-meeting details. The reasons might include, for example, participants who do not want to participate, someone with a hidden agenda, the wrong people "at the table," and perhaps a lack of leadership manifesting itself in a meeting that seems out of control. There are several communication strategies that you, as meeting leader, can use to help meetings flow smoothly and be successful. These techniques include active listening, clarification, summarizing, acknowledging the intensity of feelings or emotions, reframing, and the use of "I" statements.

Active Listening

To listen actively, you convey interest in what you are hearing, restate the speaker's ideas, reflect the speaker's feelings, and then summarize what you are hearing: "So, you are saying that the new organizational structure is troubling you. I can see why you might feel worried about your place in the new department. Let's talk more about . . ."

Clarification

You can use open-ended questions to clarify what you are hearing. This will help you to learn more about the situation and to begin to identify issues. An open-ended question might begin with the words, "Tell me more about . . ." With clarification, it is important to focus on the issues, not the person or personality who is speaking. Be careful not to imply judgment in your questions. Try to find something of value in everything that is said.

Summarizing

Summarizing allows you to pull together all of the facts before moving on in your discussion. This helps to clarify what has been said and agreed to. It also allows the group to reach consensus and move forward or to recognize that more discussion is needed. "Before we move on, let me review what I think we've decided so far. We agreed to start the new process on February 1. Joe and Jim will work together to update our policy documents. Jerry will work with the systems office to load the new software on our computers. I will alert the other departments that February 1 is the start date. We agreed to meet once each week until February. And finally, we will assess how the new process is working on February 15. Does that cover all the details we discussed?"

Dealing with Emotions

It is important to recognize that sometimes feelings and emotions are an integral part of the message being conveyed. Acknowledging the intensity of the feelings or emotions can be helpful in understanding and resolving the issue. Acknowledging and paraphrasing, and reframing, are two communication techniques that can help with emotional messages. Reframing neutralizes the messages, making them more acceptable to the listeners. Reframing can be used to increase or decrease the emotional level and, if necessary, to remove the emotion from the content.

For example, if you hear, "There is no way we can possibly pull this off by the end of the month," you might reframe it to say, "So, you think this won't work. Why won't it?"

If you hear, "He never listens to me," you might reframe it to, "It sounds like you're frustrated with Joe."

These reframed comments will encourage the speaker to reply, possibly providing you with more information or insight into the problem. Reframing separates the person from the problem.

Acknowledging and paraphrasing is another active listening technique that allows you to let the staff person know that you heard what she said, that you understand the intensity of her feelings, and that having those feelings is okay. This technique can be difficult to master. Stating that you understand the staff member, or her problem, is not necessarily acknowledging it. There are situations in which you will not want to recognize the emotional aspect of the message. For example, your department is discussing a new work schedule that requires that more staff arrive at 7 a.m. to work on a computer upgrade. Mary, an older employee, is frustrated with Joe, a younger employee, who is always late for these early morning projects. "You cannot trust him to show up," she says. Now is not the time to acknowledge Mary's emotion. Instead, try summarizing the issue by asking the group how they can be sure everyone arrives on time to help. In these situations, it will be more effective if you use another communication technique, such as reframing or summarizing, rather than acknowledging and paraphrasing.

"I" Statements

"I" statements are used to describe your feelings, describe behavior in neutral, descriptive terms, and describe the results of the behavior. In positive situations, for example, when you are telling a staff member how much you appreciate her work, "I" statements can be very powerful motivating messages.

"I am so pleased . . . when you jump in to help plan new projects . . . because I value your opinion and experience."

"I am so glad . . . you came to the meeting and participated . . . because I know how important this issue is to you."

In negative situations, "I" statements are useful because you can convey how strongly you feel about the situation.

"I feel frustrated . . . when you forget to close out the cash register . . . because I know you are aware of the library's policy."

"I am frustrated . . . when you don't participate at meetings . . . because I know you have valuable input to share."

After the Meeting

Minutes

As soon as possible after the meeting, write and distribute meeting notes or minutes, preferably within a few days. For regular meetings with individual staff members, writing summary notes about the meeting will help you to keep track of the employee's performance. You can follow up on particular issues raised at meetings, note when to revisit a particular topic, and in general keep track of the employee's progress. Notes from meetings can be shared with the staff member, to ensure that you and the staff person have a shared understanding of the discussion from the meeting. Notes from meetings with staff members can be helpful for performance evaluation purposes, both for noting the accomplishments of a high-performing individual and for the paperwork necessary when corrective action must be taken.

For unit or department meetings, minutes help keep all staff, whether or not they attended the meeting, on track and informed. Minutes should include points raised at the meeting, key components of discussions, decisions that were made, decisions that still need to be made, tasks to be performed, staff responsible for these tasks, next steps, and so on. Sample minutes from an executive committee or library management group meeting are shown below. Only action items, decisions, and key updates are included in the minutes. Distributing the meeting minutes promptly is important, both for you as a supervisor so that you can manage the activities and work of your unit and for staff members who may need reminders about the activities taking place in the unit or organization and their own role in the process. As the supervisor, you are responsible for the necessary follow-up to the meeting. You make sure that staff understand their responsibilities and carry them out. Figure 14.2 shows sample meeting minutes.

Follow-Up after Meetings

For meetings where your purpose was to gather input or brainstorm ideas, it is critical that you relay to individuals who participated the decisions made and the results of the meeting. You should explain why you have decided whatever you decided and why some ideas or suggestions that were raised cannot be implemented at this time. This will help staff to realize that their participation and input is valued and that while you

---

FIGURE 14.2   SAMPLE MEETING MINUTES

REFERENCE COMMITTEE MINUTES, NO. 201
MARCH 16

1. Minutes
The minutes to the March 2 Reference Committee meeting were approved.

2. Library Storage Facility Update
Construction bids for the facility will likely go out mid- to late April. Librarians are working on selection of titles in preparation for closing branch libraries. Initial selections are due May 1.

3. Revised Computer Rotation
Discussed the updated computer rotation schedule for workstations in library.

4. Hours
Library hours were reviewed. Based on patron usage counts, the current hours schedule will remain effective for the next year.

5. Distribution of Minutes
Reference Committee minutes will be distributed electronically only.

6. Student Budgets
E-mail the Director's Office by March 23 if you have student assistant money that you will not be using this fiscal year.

7. Announcements
The next committee meeting will be April 6.

cannot implement all of their ideas all of the time, you appreciate their time, effort, and creativity.

Benefits of Meetings

Meetings provide a mechanism for sharing information, decision making, problem solving, idea generation or brainstorming, and team building, to name just a few of the benefits. With the increasing ease of use of e-mail in libraries for communication purposes, it may be tempting to forgo scheduling at least some meetings with staff. While it is not a good idea to meet just for the sake of meeting, meetings do indicate to your staff that you value their input and contributions to the unit and organization and that you find meeting with them in person to be useful in your management of the unit. Take care to consider carefully whether meeting in person is appropriate and necessary. If there is a clear need, schedule the meeting. If not, an alternative to a group meeting that will take care of the issue may be more appropriate.

Summary

In conclusion, keep in mind the following basic tenets of good meetings.

As the meeting leader, you will

distribute the agenda in advance

set goals and discussion time limits for each agenda item

start on time

stay on task

end on time

disseminate minutes in a timely manner

As leader, you encourage all participants to

come to the meeting prepared

remember that only one person speaks at a time

participate but not dominate

respect differences

expect differences

disagree in a respectful manner

NOTES

1. Myrna J. McCallister and Thomas H. Patterson, "Conducting Effective Meetings," in *Practical Help for New Supervisors,* ed. Joan Giesecke (Chicago: American Library Association, 1997), 58.
2. Joan Giesecke, *Practical Strategies for Library Managers* (Chicago: American Library Association, 2001), 34–35.
3. Barbara I. Dewey and Sheila D. Creth, *Team Power: Making Library Meetings Work* (Chicago: American Library Association, 1993), 28.

Managing Rewards

FINDING WAYS TO reward employees, beyond the traditional reward structure of salaries and wages, has never been easy. Sometimes library budgets are determined by the larger organization (college or university, school board, library board, etc.), and supervisors may have little control over how extra funds are determined and distributed.

Salaries and Monetary Incentives

Policies for how salaries are distributed may be determined outside of the library, they may be part of a union contract, or they may be part of an overall organizational system. As a supervisor, you will want to know if people are rewarded for performance in the form of merit increases or if raises are automatic, as in cost-of-living increases or increases based on seniority. If performance is the basis for merit increases, then be sure you are conducting appropriate performance appraisals, documenting good performance as well as performance problems. Be fair to your staff by making sure that you follow organizational rules in performance procedures, so that your staff will qualify for and be recognized with merit salary increases.

Salary increases alone are not sufficient to serve as monetary rewards and incentives for encouraging and celebrating good performance. As a supervisor, you will want to explore what other options you have for recognizing outstanding performance, celebrating success, and encouraging each employee to do the best he or she can.

Some libraries will have reward structures, incentives, or bonus plans and awards already in place. Check to see if your library has policies on rewarding employees. An example of a library incentive plan is found in figure 15.1.

Review award options that exist and remember to nominate your staff for awards when appropriate. Even if staff do not win, most staff will be pleased that you took the initiative to submit a nomination.

Nonmonetary Rewards

In times of tight budgets or budget cuts, rewarding employees with monetary awards may not be possible. When funding is an issue, consider nonmonetary rewards.

There are many examples of nonmonetary rewards that you can use to recognize your employees. Not all rewards will fit with your organization. Look for rewards that blend well with library policies and unit culture. Nonmonetary rewards can include such efforts as flexible scheduling, job design, celebrations, and awards.[1]

Flexible scheduling. Flexible scheduling allows employees to plan work schedules around other factors in their lives. With many libraries open more than forty hours per week, staff may have a variety of options available to them to schedule their workweek. When available, work with staff to find schedules that match both staff needs and unit needs. Finding a schedule that works for you, your staff member, and your unit can help a staff member feel valued and be more productive.

Job design. Job enrichment, job sharing, and job rotation are all options you can use to give a person new challenges and help her learn new skills. In job enrichment, a staff member may take on new responsibilities or special projects. These challenges may be assigned as recognition of outstanding performance on the basic job tasks. In job rotation, staff may exchange positions for a limited time to have the opportunity to try new tasks. In job sharing, two staff may share a position or set up tasks so that they have time to handle other duties or work part-time. In reviewing job design options, be sure you offer opportunities fairly to your staff and do not show favoritism. Everyone who is performing well should have an opportunity to try those different task options.

Celebrations. One way to recognize outstanding performance is to celebrate successes. Celebrations can range from elaborate recognition ceremonies to a quick unit coffee break to saying thank-you to a staff member or team. While formal events provide a more structured approach that

FIGURE 15.1   INCENTIVE AWARD POLICY

THE GUIDING PRINCIPLES OF INCENTIVE AWARDS FOR THE UNIVERSITY LIBRARIES

University of Nebraska–Lincoln, October 1999

Link Incentive Awards to the Libraries' mission and goals. Incentive Award decisions must support the University Libraries' goals and values.

Base on prospective or future performance. Incentive Awards are given for prospective work and reward objective, measurable outcomes.

Provide equity in the distribution of Incentive Awards. All regular employees in the Office/ Service and Managerial/Professional classifications should be given equal opportunity to be rewarded for the results of their work. Faculty members are not eligible to receive Incentive Awards.

Give Incentive Awards for specific achievements. Actions that produce positive results, rather than subjective feelings and visibility, should be rewarded.

Hold supervisors accountable for using Incentive Awards to achieve or recognize results. Employees feel strongly that supervisors should be responsible for ensuring recognition is linked to positive actions and contributions.

Give Incentive Awards in a timely manner. Employees feel that recognition given in a timely manner is most effective.

Encourage both individual and group Incentive Awards. Group awards encourage teamwork and foster the cooperation needed to address the many complex issues faced by the Libraries.

Give employees a choice in the type of Incentive Award. Whenever possible, recipients should be allowed a choice in the type of award they receive.

Publicize Incentive Awards. The Libraries must be open in publicizing who receives Incentive Awards.

Provide flexibility for Incentive Award programs at the department level.

Provide training for supervisors and staff in effective use of Incentive Awards. A discussion of the recognition process should be included with training for new supervisors.

Periodically monitor and evaluate the Incentive Award program. Report and keep statistics on an annual basis.

Incentive Award programs are subject to change or discontinuation at the option of the University Libraries and/or the University of Nebraska–Lincoln.

Remember that for any reward to be successful, you want to be sure it is tied to performance. You will find that you see the behaviors you reward. Be sure you reward the behaviors that you want to see in your unit.

recognizes unusual efforts, quick celebrations can also help staff understand that outstanding effort will be recognized.

Awards. Many libraries have annual recognition awards to acknowledge staff excellence. These awards highlight the accomplishments of staff throughout the year and over time. Learn the criteria for these awards and share them with your staff so they can see how they can qualify for these awards.

Within the unit, you and your staff can create ways to recognize each other's work. Giving awards for new ideas, for suggestions that improve workflow, or for ideas that save money are just a few ways you can show staff that you value their efforts.

Be sure that you do not overuse awards. You want to promote and recognize desired behaviors and be sure that the performance warrants a reward, not try to give everyone an award every month.

Figure 15.2 lists the various options for nonmonetary rewards.

FIGURE 15.2   NONCASH INCENTIVE AWARDS

- Time off with pay (one to forty hours)
- Tickets to a local performance (may include movie, theater, sports event, etc.)
- Gift certificates
- Computer accessories, software, or equipment
- Office equipment
- Professional development funds
- Parking permit for one year
- Campus recreation membership
- Other choices to be determined by the employee, supervisor, and library director
- Flexible scheduling (flextime, flexitour, variable day, variable week, etc.)
- Job design (job rotation and job enrichment or enlargement)
- Celebrations of milestones on the job
- Providing desirable committee appointments or related assignments
- Asking the employee to represent the library at professional functions
- Asking the employee to accompany you to appropriate business meetings
- Extending an invitation to coauthor a publication or to work jointly on a special initiative

Generational Issues and Rewards

Changes in the demographics of the workforce complicate the reward structure. Traditional rewards no longer motivate all employees. Recognizing and understanding generational differences may help you, in your supervisory role, to provide meaningful monetary and nonmonetary rewards for employees.

Writers and researchers on multigenerational differences have varying opinions on the number of generations currently living and the characteristics that distinguish them. The generation of people born before 1924, age eighty and up in 2004 and largely not members of the current workforce, are often called Matures. The Veteran generation, born between 1925 and 1945, is also known as the World War II Generation and Traditionalists; many Veteran have retired, but others are still working. Baby Boomers, or Boomers, were born between 1946 and 1963. Sometimes people born between 1962 and 1965 are called Cuspers because they were born in the years overlapping Baby Boomers and Generation X. Generation X, born between 1964 and 1979, is sometimes called the 13th Generation. Generation Y members were born between 1980 and 1994 and have many names: Millennials, Generation Why?, Echo Boomers, 14th Generation, Y2Kids, Internet Generation, NetGeners or N-Gen, and Netizens. Members of Generation Z, born after 1994, are not yet working in libraries but will be soon.[2]

Although the year ranges may shift slightly, and names and titles vary, library employees currently belong to one of four main generational groups: Veterans, Baby Boomers, Generation X, and Generation Y.

Libraries, like other organizations and businesses, employ many Baby Boomers. In fact, Baby Boomers are the largest generation in the workforce today, with approximately 60.5 million workers in 1999 compared to 40 million Generation Xers in the same year.[3] However, researchers believe that Generation Y will become the largest generation ever.[4] Over the next few years, employers will need to rethink the traditional reward structure, adjusting to the increasingly Gen X and Gen Y workforce. While generational differences may influence the rewards desired by your employees, be careful not to let the stereotypes of each group determine reward options. Balancing the reward needs of four generations sounds impossible, but it does not have to be. Ask your staff what motivates them. You may be surprised by their answers.

Younger workers, for example, those born after 1963, might appreciate nonmonetary incentives or rewards such as increased responsibility, exposure to decision makers, or more control over their own schedules.[5] Adding supervision of student workers to a staff person's job description might be a reward to an employee wanting to build her skill set. An informal meeting with the library director, and the chance to tell the director about his new idea for streamlining the e-journal cataloging process, might be greatly appreciated by a technical services worker in a large library. The opportunity to work from home one day a week or to work a nontraditional schedule (10 a.m. to 7 p.m. instead of 8 a.m. to 5 p.m.) may help retain a high performer during years of lean raises.

If funding is available, consider purchasing rewards for these employees rather than distributing a cash bonus. Generation X and Generation Y employees may view additional training opportunities as a very worthwhile reward. If the training is job-related, the library will benefit as well. High-tech equipment, which is job-related and which the employee would enjoy learning about and using, could also benefit the library. For example, providing an iPhone for a library staff member working in your media lab so that she can use the latest web technologies would be a great reward. She has a cool iPhone for her personal and work use, and you have a happy employee with experience using the tools that your library patrons are also using.

Generation Y employees want to feel that their work has meaning: that they are making a difference. As a supervisor, you will need to find ways to convey to these young employees that their work does matter.

For Generation X, freedom and balance are key. Xers want balance in their lives. They will work hard, and in return they will feel rewarded by time off and flexible retirement options.

Baby Boomers want recognition. Boomers want to work hard and do a good job, just like their Veteran or Traditionalist predecessors and parents, but they also want everyone to know how well they did it, whatever it is. They want the salary increase, company car, better shift, and so on, the proverbial corner office with a view. While most libraries do not provide company cars, the other examples, particularly office space and work shifts, do fit.

The expression "Hard work is its own reward" is familiar to most of us, even if we heard it from a parent rather than a coworker. For Veterans, hard work is the ultimate reward. As the Veteran generation ages, libraries might want to consider rewarding them with part-time, flextime, or work-from-home scheduling. Veteran employees will feel rewarded by being needed and valued in the workplace. Other traditional rewards such as a coffee mug, plaque, or letter from the boss are also appreciated by this age group.

For groups, teams, and committees, the reward system should be tied to the group's goals and deadlines. When rewarding group members, identify the rewards that will motivate them, both individually and as a group, and then find ways to provide immediate rewards. For a team with members from multiple generations, offer a smorgasbord of rewards and let individuals choose. Rewarding the team as they make progress when they reach a milestone or meet a deadline will motivate them to continue with the project.

For example, Tony heads a large cataloging department in a library that restructured, merging the serials and acquisitions departments into the cataloging department. The new department is composed primarily of Baby Boomers with 75 percent of the staff in the Baby Boomer generation, 15 percent in the Veterans group, 5 percent in Generation X, and 5 percent in Generation Y. Tony is a Gen Xer who does not have much experience supervising Baby Boomers, although he has worked with them for several years. He wants to set up a system to recognize staff who help develop procedures that will significantly streamline workflow and free up staff to work on special projects. His library has an incentive program to reward performance on task forces and projects. Tony decides to use the incentive program to encourage staff to look creatively at the workflow. He calls a department meeting to announce the program. He plans to award an extra vacation day to staff who propose ideas that are then implemented. His plan is met by silence. Tony is confused. What went wrong? Why isn't his department energized by the plan? After the meeting, Tony talks to a few of his staff individually to get their reaction. He hears from two staff members in the Veteran generation that they don't see any reason to reward ideas that should just be part of what good staff do. Why reward work that should be done anyway? Wouldn't a simple thank-you say it all? Tony finds that his Gen X colleagues like the idea of extra vacation days. They are already dreaming up plans to overhaul the unit. The Baby Boomers are not engaged in the project. Tony talks to a close friend in this generation, who points out that not only do the majority of the department's members expect to be included in the original planning of the incentive program, but that the incentives should include public recognition and acknowledgment of each person's role. Taking an extra vacation day may be pleasant, but it is not enough of an incentive to do the extra work.

Tony needs to regroup. He can give the department an opportunity to modify the plan. He can include a project-end celebration and recognition party along with the incentive. He can give staff a choice of two or three incentives rather than expecting everyone to want the same thing. By working with different members of the department, Tony can create a program to recognize and reward staff in ways that will be meaningful to most staff members.

Figure 15.3 summarizes different reward approaches for different generations.

FIGURE 15.3   DIFFERENT REWARDS FOR DIFFERENT GENERATIONS

Veterans/Traditionalists

- Handwritten thank-you note
- Plaque
- Photo of themselves with the library director (or college president, library board president, important visitor, etc.)
- Alternate scheduling
- Job security

Baby Boomers

- Time (errand service, dry cleaning pickup, etc.)
- Promotion and new job title
- Cash bonus
- Expensive symbolic gift (Rolex watch, etc.)
- Rewards that contribute toward plan for same standard of living at retirement
- Retirement and financial counseling

Generation X

- Challenging work
- Higher salary and better benefits
- Flexibility and freedom (work schedule)
- Daily proof that work matters
- Involvement in decision-making process
- Managers who allow flexibility and creativity
- Evidence of rewards tied directly to performance
- Clear areas of responsibility

Generation Y/Millennials/Nexters

- Meaningful work
- Learning opportunities
- Time for personal or family activities
- A fun place to work
- Desire for autonomy
- Want to be treated like a colleague, not a kid
- Fairness and fair play in the workplace

Summary

Appropriately rewarding and recognizing staff is an important component of the overall system for encouraging top performance by your staff. Recognition programs should allow for different ways to reward staff members and should include a range of activities, from formal events to handwritten thank-you notes.

NOTES

1. Irene M. Padilla and Thomas H. Patterson, "Rewarding Employees Nonmonetarily," in *Practical Help for New Supervisors,* ed. Joan Giesecke (Chicago: American Library Association, 1997), 36–38.
2. Scott Hays, "Generation X and the Art of the Reward," *Workforce* 11 (November 1999): 46; Lynne C. Lancaster and David Stillman, *When Generations Collide: Who They Are, Why They Clash; How to Solve the Generational Puzzle at Work* (New York: HarperCollins, 2002); Sue Schlichtemeier-Nutzman, presentation on multigenerational diversity for University Libraries, University of Nebraska–Lincoln, 2001.
3. Hays, "Generation X," 46.
4. Mark L. Alch, "Get Ready for a New Type of Worker in the Workplace: The Net Generation," *Supervision* 61 (April 2000): 3–7.
5. Ron Zemke, Claire Raines, and Bob Bilipczak, *Generations at Work: Managing the Clash of Veterans, Boomers, Xers, and Nexters in Your Workplace* (New York: AMACOM, 1999).

Project Management

GINA, THE HEAD of the reference department, arrives at work one day to find out that the head of collection development has taken a leave of absence just as he was ready to head a journal cancellation project. Gina is asked to step in and head a team to plan and identify 10 percent of the journal collection that can be eliminated in order to balance the budget. The team will have six months to consult with interested groups and identify a clean list of titles that will be canceled. Every department in the library is impacted by this budget problem, from selectors to reference staff to the technical services and systems staff. How will Gina go about ensuring that all these stakeholders are involved and yet meet the short deadline for this project? Gina could decide to make all the decisions herself, but she knows that will not be effective. For one thing, she is not a subject expert in every area and she does not know all the intricacies of the various electronic licenses, package plans, and consortium purchases that determine what titles can actually be eliminated. Moreover, this is not the first time the library has had to cancel journals, and she understands that the simpler decisions have already been made. This time, the library will be cutting core titles. What will Gina do? How can she organize this work and meet the deadline? Gina decides to have coffee with her colleague Tony, head of cataloging, to get some ideas on how to proceed. Tony suggests using project management processes to carry out this assignment. Gina asks, "What are project management processes, and how do I use them on this assignment?"

Project Management Overview

The above scenario is not all that unusual in today's libraries. Supervisors and managers may find themselves called upon to head interdepartmental projects or organization-wide task forces. When these assignments involve a project with a defined beginning and end, you may want to use a formal project management structure to organize and carry out the assignment. Project management is used extensively in the information technology field, where implementing new systems or resolving problems are often done as projects. Using a formal project management process will help you plan, organize, manage, and deliver projects with defined outcomes.[1]

Before you accept the assignment to head a project management work team, you will want to determine if project management is an appropriate process to use to structure the work. Are you being given a true project as the assignment? A project is a planned undertaking and set of related activities that has a defined beginning and end. It is often an interdepartmental undertaking that includes resources that go beyond one department. The scope of the project often impacts many parts of the organization. While you can use a project management process within your department, you may find it most helpful when working between organizational units.

The Players

There are a number of people or stakeholders inside and outside of the organization that will be part of a project. Each group has a defined role in the process. Management is responsible for identifying projects, assigning priorities to projects, identifying the project manager, and providing ongoing support. At the end of the project, management is responsible for recognizing and rewarding the project manager and team.

The sponsor of the project is the member of the management team who authorizes the project, grants the project manager the authority to complete the project, and supports the project manager throughout the life of the project. The sponsor is responsible for finding the resources needed by the team to accomplish the charge.

The project manager is the person who heads the project team and controls the processes that make the project happen. The project manager negotiates for time and resources needed by the team. Being a project manager can turn into a full-time job. The project manager needs to negotiate for changes in his work assignments in order to be sure he has the time to devote to the project.

The project team consists of the people responsible for doing the work. These people are chosen, based on the skills needed by the team, by the project manager to carry out the charge to the group.

Customers or users are the groups that will in some way be impacted by the outcomes of the project. In the journal cancellation project, users can include the faculty and students in a school or academic environment, the library users in a public setting, or the members of a company for a special library.

As part of the planning process, the project team will want to be sure to identify as many of the stakeholders as they can. This way, the team can be sure that groups that need to be consulted or informed about the project will receive appropriate and timely communication.

Managing the Project Process

There are four phases to a project: initiation, planning, execution, and closedown. It is important to be sure to go through all four phases, including closing down the project, in order to have a successful project.

Project Initiation

In the initial phase of the project, the size, scope, and complexity of the project are identified. As the project manager, you will want to use this time to establish the parameters of the project, establish the project team, and negotiate your authority, your time commitment, and the resources you will have available to you. For your own survival, be sure you negotiate which of your regular responsibilities you will not be fulfilling so that you will have time to devote to the project.

Choosing your project team is a crucial step in creating a successful venture. Work with the sponsor of the project to identify the skills that are needed. Then choose members of the organization who have the skills you need. Look for people who can complement your strengths.

Review the charge to the team with the sponsor. Be sure you understand exactly what is being asked of the group and agree to the outcomes. How will you know if you are successful? For the journal cancellation project, be sure you know exactly what journal cost total is 10 percent of the budget. Because journal costs change every year, be sure you agree on how you will determine the subscription cost for a given title. Iron out any differences now before you begin the project. This will avoid problems later.

Outline the steps needed to begin the project. Who needs to be contacted as part of the initiation phase? How will you report to the sponsor and other members of the management group? How will you assign roles to team members? How will you work with the sponsor if changes are needed in the project? What type of funding can you expect for the project? These are the kinds of questions you will want to be sure are answered as part of the initiation phase.

Finally, in this initial stage, establish how you will keep track of the correspondence, activities, and deliverables that are part of the project. Creating a project notebook, either in print or online, can help you keep the group and the procedures organized. It will be important to record decisions made throughout the process, communications sent, and reports submitted. Establishing how you will document your progress now will make it easier to keep track of the project throughout the life of the team.

Project Planning

There are six basic steps for planning a project: defining the objectives, structuring the project, scheduling the project, analyzing the plan for risks, reviewing the plan for assumptions, and establishing controls.

Define the objectives. Define the scope of the project. What is the problem to be solved? What are the deliverables for this project and how will they be measured? How will you know when the project is finished? These questions need to be answered as a first step in the planning process. In the journal cancellation project, you will want to know what needs to be included in the list of journals. Do you need ISSN numbers, costs, publisher information, vendors, or just a list of journal titles? Will the list be in a spreadsheet format, done from an online system, or handwritten? Working out these details now will help ensure that you do not need to redo work once it is done.

Structure the project. Now is the time to divide the project into manageable tasks. Identify the tasks to be accomplished and the order in which the tasks will be done. These are known as work breakdown structures and help you develop a logical approach to the work that will need to be done.

Part of the planning process includes developing a communication plan. Often this is the step we are most likely to skip or do quickly. However, having a well-thought-out communication plan can be the difference between successful projects and projects with problems. In the communication plan, include when and how reports on progress will be given and to whom. How will stakeholders be consulted? Will publicity for the project be needed? If so, who will do the publicity and when? In the journal cancellation project, plan how you will announce the project to your constituencies. How will you alert users that journals will be canceled? How will you keep members of the staff informed of your progress so they can answer questions from patrons about the project? The more you communicate and follow a careful plan for communicating, the fewer problems you will have with misinformation getting out and rumors destroying your progress or credibility.

Schedule the project. Now that you have the tasks identified, estimate the resources you will need to accomplish the tasks. Resources include staff time as well as budget resources, supplies, and equipment needed for the project. Also identify the amount of time needed for each task. Some tasks may need to be accomplished before others can begin. Some tasks may be done simultaneously. Some tasks may be accomplished more quickly by increasing the resources devoted to the task. Identify those tasks that are most critical and be sure you have allowed enough time to accomplish these activities. Get agreement for the budget and time line from your sponsor or management group.

Assess risks. Now that you have the tasks listed and a schedule in mind, assess the risks involved in the project. What happens if an internal deadline is missed? How likely is it that supplies or equipment could be delayed? How likely is it that the project will result in adverse publicity for the organization? How can you decrease the chances of various problems occurring? Are there things you can do in your plan to decrease any particular risk from becoming a problem?

Review the plan for assumptions. Can the time line be met? Are the resources you need available? Can the work be done as outlined in the plan? Think about the assumptions you made when developing the task list and be sure those assumptions are still valid.

Establish controls. Negotiate the budget and the plan with management. Review the key statement of work with the sponsor and be sure that the key stakeholders have a clear understanding of what you plan to do and how you plan to do it. Be sure everyone understands the project size, duration, and outcomes. Finally, determine how you will make changes in the plan as needed and how you will keep the sponsor and management group informed of changes as they occur.

Once you have reviewed and agreed to a plan of action, you are ready to execute the project.

Project Execution

Now is the time to follow your plan. Initiate activities, assign resources, train staff as needed, and make sure that quality measures are being met. You may need to do some team building here to be sure that those involved in the project work well together as a team that is dependent on each member in meeting their assignments.

Monitor progress on each task and be sure your team members are doing the work they said they would do. Continually compare progress on activities to the baseline plan and be sure you are on target. Adjust resource allocations as needed if budgets get ahead or behind schedule. Reassign personnel if needed to meet the project deadlines.

Make changes and adjustments as needed to keep the project on track. You may need to change specifications, internal deadlines, or redo activities if a task gets bungled. Also, identify new activities that may be needed but were not anticipated in the planning process. For example, in the journal cancellation project, you may need to add in meetings with interested faculty if you had not included those initially and faculty become more concerned than anticipated. Finally, decide what to do if an activity is delayed. Can you rearrange tasks, adjust schedules, or move resources to bring the project back on track? Be sure you are maintaining the project workbook and documenting progress throughout.

Project Closedown

You have finished your tasks, met your deadlines, and are ready to end the project. Be sure you formally close down the project so everyone will know that you are done. Notify stakeholders that the project is concluded and deliverables have been finished. Work with management and customers to assess the strengths and weaknesses of the deliverables. Have you provided the final product that was needed? Can the organization use the work you did?

In addition to ending the tasks, you need to close down the team. Assess the team members and support their transitions back to their regular jobs. Finalize documentation and submit budget reports that are required. And most important, celebrate your success. You have done a great job and deserve to celebrate that success. The celebration is also a way for the organization to thank all of the team members for their help in making the project a success.

Simplified Project Management

The project management process can be simplified to be used to help organize multistep projects. For example, in the scenario of a serials cancellation project, a simplified project management process can be used by technical services to design workflow to cancel the many subscriptions that are being dropped. In order to cancel numerous subscriptions, the technical services unit will have to verify all the titles to be canceled, review and modify the various order and serial records, notify vendors and publishers, and be sure the public catalog accurately reflects the revised holdings for the library. Each of these activities includes a number of steps that must occur, and the steps need to be performed in the correct order for the records to be modified correctly and to avoid duplicate work. These types of projects, with multiple steps and multiple deadlines, lend themselves to a project planning process.

To see how the simplified process can work, let us revisit Tony and his colleagues in technical services. They face the challenge of determining how best to cancel the journal subscriptions and revise all of the appropriate records so that the library does not pay for titles that it no longer wishes to receive. The head of technical services puts together a small project team to oversee the records project. In the first meeting, the group determines the steps that are needed to verify that the titles can be canceled (i.e., are not part of package plans or are multiyear subscriptions), close the order records, revise all related records, and notify the vendors and publishers. For each activity, the group determines who can help with the project, what resources are needed, and what equipment will be needed. The group then sets deadlines based on the timing of invoices. All records need to be revised prior to the receipt of the serial renewal invoices. Using backward planning, the group assigns deadlines to each step to ensure that the project ends on time.

There are also a number of planning techniques that can be used by the group to break down the workflow for the project.[2] Gantt charts provide a graphic way to outline the progress of activities and to avoid overlapping deadlines. Program Evaluation and Review Technique or critical path analysis is a technique that helps planners determine the order in which activities need to occur for the project to be successful. Even relatively simple Excel spreadsheets can help the team keep track of activities, deadlines, and progress on the project.

Once the team outlines the steps in the process and identifies who can help with each step, the planning group notes how the work will be revised and evaluated and how success will be measured. Because a project such as a serials cancellation project could easily involve all members of technical services departments, including staff who may not have much experience with serial records, the team must remember to include time to train staff to complete the records revision activities.

As the above shows, taking an organized approach to planning—carefully listing out the many activities needed to complete a large project, assigning tasks to individuals, assigning deadlines, ensuring that evaluation occurs throughout the project, and revising plans if needed as the project continues—increases the chances that the project will be successfully completed.

Summary

By following a formal planning and project process, you can manage both large and small projects and bring them to successful outcomes. Skipping steps or cutting short the process will increase the chances of failure. Instead, take the time needed to do the project correctly and thoroughly. In the end, you will save time and resources that would be needed to redo the work. Project management can be very satisfying and fun. When done well it can help you accomplish complex, interdepartmental tasks and show management that you are a successful project manager.

NOTES

1. There are numerous books that outline the formal project management process. For an overview of the process, see Patricia Buhler, *Alpha Teach Yourself Management Skills in 24 Hours* (Indianapolis: Alpha Books, 2001), 83–98; and George M. Doss, *IS Project Management Handbook* (New York: Prentice Hall, 2000).
2. Bob Pymm and Damon Hickey, *Learn Library Management,* 2nd ed. (Friendswood, TX: Total Recall, 2007).

Career Management

WHILE YOU ARE busy supporting the development of your staff and helping them plan their careers, it is important to take time to plan your own career. But before you sigh and decide this is one more ball you don't want to juggle, take a moment to think about where you are in your career and where you want to be. Even if you have addressed your career goals, it's important to be aware of changes in the field, in your organization, and in your life that can impact your position and change how you feel about your career. Keeping an eye on your career can help you achieve balance in your personal and your work life.

Overview

Career management has changed. In the last generation, a career implied working for one organization. Employees spent thirty or more years with the same organization or system and did not consider changing jobs. Today, we live in a world where many of our staff will have three or four careers and will move among fields. Job switching is becoming more common. Employees look for ways to stay engaged, refreshed, and challenged. If their current job does not keep them excited, they leave. You may feel the same way. If so, you can take steps to keep your career moving forward.

Stages of Career Development

Traditionally, careers proceeded through the following stages: exploration, organizational entry, establishment, maintenance, and finally disengagement.[1] You started by learning about a career area, usually through higher education options. Perhaps you worked in a library as a student. You found out more about the field and the job options for librarians and information scientists.

Next, you find a job in this field. The challenge here is to match your own interests and skills with that of an employer. Finding a satisfying first job can be a real challenge. Once the first job is acquired, you need to build the skills that will make you a valuable employee.

As time goes on, you will reach a mid-career level. Here is a time to assess where you are in your career. Are you satisfied with the skills you have? Do you enjoy what you do? If not, it's time to make changes. If you are satisfied with your career, then be sure to examine how you can keep your skills current and continue to grow in our rapidly changing information environment.

The final stage of a career is retirement or disengagement. Here you want to look at what new things you want to do and how you will change your life for either retirement or a new career.

While these are the traditional steps in career development, people entering the workforce now may have three, four, or more careers. Their planning time frame will be shorter, but they will still experience these five stages of career development.

Nonlinear Career Paths

The above process is a linear approach to career development. It looks good on paper, but it may not relate to your experience. Instead, we need to recognize that there are a variety of career paths for us. These include upward mobility, project management, resource provider, and technical advancement.[2]

Upward mobility is the traditional career path for managers. You start as a first-time supervisor and advance through the management ranks. This path still exists, but the number of positions in this path are decreasing. As organizations merge, restructure, and downsize, management opportunities are eliminated. As a manager, you will want to carefully watch what is happening to jobs in your area and prepare for changes.

Project management provides a different advancement option for today's supervisors. Project managers oversee significant projects and contribute to the success of the organization. Leading projects can be a way to advance in your organization even though you do not head a unit or department.

Obtaining financial resources is another career opportunity. These are the people who manage and obtain resources and oversee the human relations aspects of the organization. This staff function can be a career advancement opportunity.

Technical expertise is another way to promote advancement. Technical experts possess knowledge skills and abilities that help the organization remain technologically current and advance in this changing aspect of our field.[3]

Plateaus

Career plateaus can occur even when you have carefully planned your approach to career development. Structural plateaus occur when there are no promotional opportunities left in your current organization. Here, your option for upward mobility is limited to finding positions in other organizations.[4]

Content plateaus occur when you have mastered the tasks of your position and find you have no more challenges. Content plateaus are less likely to occur in the information field, where changes in technology and in information resources add interest and change to our positions. Opportunities for learning abound in our field.

Another source of plateauing can occur when we feel we can no longer advance and see this lack of change as a failure in our lives. Staff who measure their self-worth by their jobs can be vulnerable to such feelings. As a manager, you will want to be sure you do not become so focused on your job that you neglect other areas of your life.

Personal Guidance

To manage your career, you should decide where you want to go and then design strategies to get there. You may want to carry out your own strategic planning process for your career.

Begin with a vision just as you do for your organization or unit. Describe what kinds of positions you want. Where do you want to be in five or ten years? What aspects of the information field are most exciting to you? What jobs do you see around you that look interesting and exciting?

Decide, too, what kinds of organizations you want to work in. Do you prefer small organizations, multibranch systems, large organizations, or commercial, nonprofit, or public institutions? Thinking through the characteristics of an organization that is important to you will help you as you map out your career.

Next, it's time to do your own SWOT analysis of your strengths, weaknesses, opportunities, and threats. Look at what skills you have and which ones you need to develop. Think about the options you have to build your career and the barriers that can slow your progress.

Use this information to help focus your planning so you can capitalize on opportunities as they arrive. Look for projects that will help you gain experience and round out your skill set. Add to and refine your options as you assess changes that can impact your own goals.

Finally, stay flexible. The information field is always changing. Jobs change and organizations change. If you are too rigid in your planning, you may miss opportunities to advance or may become stuck in a dead-end position.

Avoiding Dead Ends

You can work to avoid dead-end positions if you keep your eyes open and pay attention to how the field is developing.[5]

Trends. Keep up with the literature about the information field. Read what trends, changes, and new options are developing. By staying aware of how the field is changing, you can assess how you can use these changes to your advantage.

Technology. Keep current on technology changes. As our patrons move from computers to laptops to PDAs for their information, we need to move with them. Even if your library isn't keeping up with the latest technology and software advances, you need to be aware of these changes. By keeping your skills current, you will stay more employable and better able to control your own career options.

Networking. You also want to be sure you continue to network with colleagues, managers, vendors, and others even as you move through management positions. Your personal network can help you assess your career options as well as help alert you to changes that may be harmful to your own advancement.

Mergers and reorganizations. Finally, be aware that mergers and reorganizations can occur and can change the direction your career is taking. Library systems can merge, and certain types of libraries are now merging or downsizing. Schools and corporations may be eliminating their libraries. While you cannot anticipate every possible change, you can stay prepared for changes by watching for signs of economic problems and by watching how top decision makers are assessing the organization. As you learn to read between the lines on announcements of changes, you can prepare yourself for then. By keeping your skills up-to-date and your options open, you will have a better chance of surviving an economic downturn or major restructuring effort.

Personal Balance

While you are working on your career plans, you should also look at how to achieve a balance in your life. Personal wellness, family health, and work effectiveness are all related. You are more effective at work when you take care of your own well-being and develop a positive life outside of your job.[6]

You can apply the same planning techniques you use to assess your career to planning your personal life. Begin by identifying your personal values. Decide what things are most important to you. Think about how you rank social interactions, friends, family, religious values, a home, time for recreation, and so on. Decide, too, how you like to spend your time. How much time do you want or need for work, sleep, social activities, home maintenance, and so on? Putting these two lists together will help you focus your time.

Next, set realistic goals for yourself, given the things you need to do and want to do. Use these goals to design your own personal action plan of how you will spend your time. If refereeing your children's softball games is a high priority, then look at how to arrange your job so you have time to be a referee. If serving on a local charity board is a goal, think about what steps you need to take to become a member of the board.

And then leave yourself time for fun and relaxation. Try to remember that you cannot control every minute of your day. Do take time to enjoy yourself, to refresh and relax. This time will help you stay refreshed and more able to cope with the challenges at work and in your personal life.

If you are having trouble doing planning by yourself, consider talking to a human resource person at work for ideas. Your institution may have offices that assist with career planning. There are also community-based services available. A life coach can help you set boundaries and create a balanced life. Some health clubs have courses to help you with life-planning issues. Look around your area and find resources that can help you as you plan your career and your life.

Managing Stress

No matter how well you take care of yourself, you will find yourself under pressure and will experience stress. One key to surviving the pressures of everyday life is to learn to manage that stress as best you can. There are numerous techniques or rules that can help you deal with stress in a constructive manner.

First, take a deep breath and recognize that you cannot always be right. Mistakes do happen. Other people have better ideas. Instead of trying to always be right, try to do your best and accept that sometimes you will not be first, nor will you always be the best.

Second, do not let stresses build up. Handle little situations as they occur to prevent large problems. For example, do not wait until the last minute to start a project. Set up a time line that lets you work on a project and allows for problems to arise and be handled before the deadline. By planning in time for problems, you can decrease the stress that is caused by rushing to meet a deadline when things go awry.

Last, learn what situations cause you stress and develop strategies for handling these situations. For example, if you know you become stressed if you are late for an appointment, then plan your day to try to arrive ten minutes early. That way, if something comes up that delays you, you are still likely to be on time for the meeting. By studying your own reactions to different situations, you can learn to control your own reactions and behavior. You can decrease stress by decreasing the number of times you are surprised or caught off guard.

Stress is a natural part of our lives. By learning to manage stress, you can decrease the effect stress has on your life, your health, and your work.

Summary

Remember to take time to take care of yourself and your career. Think carefully about how to balance your personal life and your work life. Develop goals and plans that help you meet your needs as you work to ensure that your staff and unit meet the organization's needs. You will not be effective if you neglect your own life, become frustrated, and get burned out. Instead, take time to reflect and plan so you can enjoy your life and your career.

NOTES
1. Patricia Buhlen, *Alpha Teach Yourself Management Skills in 24 Hours* (Indianapolis: Alpha Books, 2001), 188.
2. Ibid., 191.
3. Ibid.
4. Ibid., 190.
5. Gary McClain and Deborah S. Romaine, *The Everything Managing People Book* (Avon, MA: Adams Media, 2002), 261–81.
6. Edward Betof and Frederic Harwood, *Just Promoted! How to Survive and Thrive in Your First 12 Months as a Manager* (New York: McGraw-Hill, 1992), 233.

Index

You may also be interested in